HOW FREE SPEECH
SAVED DEMOCRACY

HOW FREE SPEECH SAVED DEMOCRACY

*The Untold History of How the First
Amendment Became an Essential Tool
for Securing Liberty and Social Justice*

By Christopher M. Finan

TRUTH TO POWER

an imprint of

STEERFORTH PRESS

LEBANON, NEW HAMPSHIRE

Cataloging-in-Publication Data is available from the Library of Congress

ISBN 978-1-58642-298-1 (Paperback)

Manufactured in the United States of America

1 3 5 7 9 10 8 6 4 2

DEDICATION

For everyone who has fought for free speech:
Abolitionists, Anarchists, Atheists, Artists, Authors,
Booksellers, Civil Libertarians, Civil Rights Activists,
Defenders of LGBTQI Rights, Feminists, "Free Lusters,"
Jehovah Witnesses, Journalists, Librarians, Librarians,
Lawyers, Parents, Publishers, Professors, Students,
Unionists, Socialists, Teachers, Wobblies,

and

Philip D. (Phil) Harvey (1938–2021),
who risked his freedom to defend the
First Amendment rights of all Americans.

CONTENTS

FOREWORD

In *How Free Speech Saved Democracy*, Chistopher M. Finan offers a brisk, concise, vivid chronicle of struggles throughout American history over claims to freedom of expression. His thesis is clear and compellingly argued: "The most important reason for defending free speech for all, including those we fear or abhor, is that history shows the power of free speech to change things for the better." In propounding this message, Finan brilliantly performs several useful tasks. For one thing, he introduces readers to unfamiliar facets of the lives of well-known figures. Frederick Douglass is famous for his abolitionist oratory and journalism. Finan highlights Douglass's eloquent, though overlooked, demands that speakers and writers be protected against censorship. "The right of speech," Douglass asserted, "is a very precious one, especially to the oppressed." Condemning a mob that broke up a meeting he was supposed to address, Douglass maintained that "to suppress free speech is a double wrong. It violates the rights of the hearer as well as those of the speaker." Similarly dedicated to freedom of expression as both ends and means was Martin Luther King Jr. In his first major speech as a civil rights leader, calling for the Black community of Montgomery, Alabama, to boycott racially segregated busses, King insisted that "the only weapon that we have in our hands is the weapon of protest." Voicing appreciation for the leeway to deploy dissent, King remarked that "the great glory of American democracy is the right to protest for the right."

Finan also accentuates obscure figures who gave their all to express themselves despite knowing that doing so would elicit painful repression. Ida C. Craddock, for example, was a mystic freethinker who offered sex counseling in the 1890s, which provoked fervent efforts to silence her. Craddock's mother succeeded briefly in committing her to an insane asylum. An employer fired her on account of her writings. She was repeatedly arrested on obscenity charges and endured imprisonment. Upon yet another conviction that carried with it a ten-year term of incarceration, Craddock committed suicide.

The executive director of the National Coalition Against Censorship (NCAC), Finan writes especially knowingly about figures who have contributed significantly to the institutional infrastructure of freedom of expression. This includes the remarkable Roger Nash Baldwin, the principal guide and inspiration behind the American Civil Liberties Union (ACLU) during its first several decades. "I am dead certain," Baldwin declared, "that human progress depends on those heretics, rebels, and dreamers . . . whose 'holy discontent' has challenged established authority and created the expanding visions mankind may yet realize." Finan's heroes also include entrepreneurs like Horace Liveright, who, as the publisher of Eugene O'Neil, Ernest Hemingway, and Theodore Dreiser, did battle against the "Clean Books League" and others who sought to repress "bad books."

Finan lauds judges like Justice Oliver Wendell Holmes Jr., who warned that "we should be eternally vigilant against attempts to check the expression of opinions that we loathe and believe to be fraught with death." Similarly, Finan praises Justice William J. Brennan, who imagined the tradition "of a profound national commitment to the principle that debate on public issues should be uninhibited, robust, and wide open . . ." Librarians receive appreciative attention in Finan's history, particularly the leadership of the American Library Association (ALA), which established in 1939 the Library's Bill of Rights. Asserting a position that is deeply controversial today, the ALA maintained that librarians should obtain books based on "value and interest" and ignore "the race or nationality or the political or religious views of the writers." Further lauding the ALA, Finan quotes a statement that it adopted in 1953 in the midst of anticommunist hysteria. Embracing "The Freedom to Read," the ALA declared: "We believe . . . that what people read is deeply important; that ideas can be dangerous; but that the suppression of ideas is fatal to a democratic society. Freedom itself is a dangerous way of life, but it is ours."

As he delineates the progressive dissenting tradition, Finan concurrently examines the partisans of repression. He soberingly beckons us to recall that on July 4, 1798, Congress enacted the Sedition Act, which threatened with imprisonment and fines anyone who said anything "false, scandalous or malicious" about federal officials in an effort to "excite against them the hatred of the people" — a vague, manipulable proscription that Federalist authorities used enthusiastically against their adversaries. Finan reminds us that anti-slavery journalists were routinely subjected to mobbing and that vigilantes issued bounties for their detention. When Elijah P. Lovejoy voiced support for gradual emancipation in Missouri, enraged opponents told him "freedom of speech and press does not imply a moral right . . . to freely discuss the subject of slavery . . . a question too nearly allied [with] the vital interests of the Slaveholding States to admit of public disputation." When Lovejoy persisted, he was made to flee, fearing for the safety of his family. Later he was murdered.

Finan insists that we remember that in 1873, Congress enacted a national censorship statute that empowered Anthony Comstock, the head of the New York Society for the Suppression of Vice, to patrol the country, threatening with prosecution purveyors of information, beliefs, or images that he perceived to be "obscene." Comstock engineered the jailing of Victoria Woodhull (the first woman to run for president) because she had the temerity to publicize the adultery of Henry Ward Beecher, one of the country's most prominent ministers. Comstock thought it scandalous that a woman would write about sexual affairs for the public and be paid for doing so. Comstock successfully prosecuted Dr. Edward Bliss Foote for mailing pamphlets that described methods of birth control; D. M. Bennett (the publisher of *The Truth Seeker* newspaper) for mailing a pamphlet, *Cupid's Yokes*, that promoted "free love" (i.e., sex outside of marriage), and Ezra Haywood for publishing a letter that contained the word *fuck*.

In the late nineteenth century, judges repeatedly issued overbroad injunctions that unfairly muzzled striking laborers. An injunction in Seattle, Washington, for example, barred strikers from "using in any way any language tending to . . . incite the antagonism of the citizens . . . and from using any language ridiculing the institutions of this country . . ." In World War I, the federal government denied mail service to purportedly "disloyal" newspapers and prosecuted thousands of dissidents under a malleable federal statute that the United States Justice Department stretched to reach even anodyne protest. The socialist leader Rose Pastor Stokes was declared a criminal for writing "I am for the people and the government is for the profiteers." During the Cold War, many officials did what they could to expose, intimidate, and ostracize dissidents who were widely denounced as "un-American." And more recently, putative guardians of decency have tried to suppress books, films, and music that they perceive as destructive to "family values" and other pillars of straight, white, middle-class conventionality.

Finan shows, in sum, that the authoritarianism so scarily present today stems, at least in part, from an entrenched tradition that has long sought to master the soul of America. He titles his project *How Free Speech Saved Democracy*. That packaging, however, is a bit more optimistic than his text. Finan argues that free speech has saved American democracy and may do so yet again *if* those who appreciate the best version of the American experiment do what is required to defend freedom of expression. A step in the right direction is to read the book that follows.

Randall Kennedy
Cambridge, Massachusetts
December 2021

INTRODUCTION

From the beginning of American history, people have used free speech to advocate for change. Often they have been people lacking political power, like the three thousand Black men and women who gathered in Philadelphia in 1817 to protest the plans of the American Colonization Society to send them "back" to Africa; or reformers who gathered in Seneca Falls, New York, in 1848 to demand that women receive equal rights, including the right to vote; or workers who fought for more than a century for the right to organize unions and strike for a living wage.

Conservatives seeking to retain power, even, or especially, when they were in the minority, have tended to fight change: Federalists who supported voting rights only for men of wealth, Democrats who defended slavery, and present-day Republicans who target people from historically marginalized groups with legislation that restricts voting rights. Defenders of slavery violently attacked abolitionists without fear of arrest or retribution. Judges threw suffragists into jail for picketing the White House and force-fed them through rubber hoses when they staged hunger strikes. Government used troops to crush strikes.

In announcing the Montgomery bus boycott in 1955, Martin Luther King Jr. explained that he intended to push the right to protest to the limit. "The only weapon that we have in our hands is the weapon of protest," he said. "If we were incarcerated behind the iron curtains of a communistic country — we couldn't do this. If we were trapped in the dungeon of a totalitarian regime — we couldn't do this. But the great glory of American democracy is the right to protest for the right."

Segregationists did everything they could to thwart civil rights protests. They launched a legal attack on the Southern Christian Leadership Conference and the National Association for the Advancement of Colored People. Police used fire hoses and attack dogs to disrupt demonstrations. The Ku Klux Klan killed civil rights workers.

As a new age of protest has dawned, the fight for social change continues. Millions of women marched a day after Donald Trump took office in 2017. Later, high school kids across the country left their classrooms to protest gun violence. The Black Lives Matter movement sent demonstrators into the streets of hundreds of communities. Protests catalyzed by the murder of George Floyd while handcuffed by police in Minneapolis were the largest in American history.

This is the story of how the powerless have used free speech to pursue the promise of equal rights for all and how it continues to fuel the fight for democracy.

1

THE MARTYR AGE

Founding Principles

Matthew Lyon spat in the face of Roger Griswold during an argument on the floor of the US House of Representatives on January 30, 1798. Griswold belonged to the party in control of the presidency and Congress, the Federalists, and Lyon was a member of the opposition, the Democratic-Republican Party.

Griswold's colleagues introduced a motion to expel Lyon. When the motion was defeated several weeks later, Griswold took matters into his own hands. Using a hickory walking stick he bought for the occasion, he attacked Lyon as he was sitting at his desk waiting for the day's session to begin.

"I called him a scoundrel & struck him with my cane, and pursued him with more than twenty blows on his head and back," Griswold wrote. When Lyon attempted to fight back with a pair of fire tongs he managed to grab, Griswold tackled him and punched him several times before his friends pulled him away.[1]

It was almost inevitable that Lyon and Griswold would come to blows. They came from different worlds.

Lyon was one of the "new men" who had risen to political prominence during the American Revolution. When he arrived in the British colonies, he was an indentured servant from Ireland. The Irish people as a whole were widely despised in America, although Lyon's lot would have been even worse had he been a Catholic.

Leaving Ireland alone at the age of fifteen to take his chances in the new world, he had succeeded against the odds. After completing his term as a servant and toiling for a brief period as a farmer, he began to purchase unclaimed land in what would become Vermont.

Lyon joined the Continental army and received an officer's commission. Following the defeat of the British, he resumed his land purchases, buying up property abandoned by those who had opposed the war. The sale of land provided the capital that he used to become a successful entrepreneur. Among other endeavors, he owned various kinds of mills and published a newspaper.

Griswold, on the other hand, descended from an aristocratic Connecticut family. The rise of men from the lower classes into political leadership offended him, as it did other Federalists. He especially despised Lyon for being Irish and for his former servitude. "[H]e is literally one of the most ignorant contemptible and brutal fellows in Congress and that is saying a great deal," Griswold wrote a friend.[2]

In light of this assessment, Griswold should have known better than to lay his hand upon the arm of Lyon, who was known to be

Griswold versus Lyon on the floor of the House of Representatives, Philadelphia, 1798

inclined to bursts of temper, and insult his war record to his face. The personal quarrel that ensued on the floor of the House set the stage for the first free speech crisis in US history.

In 1798, the US Constitution was only ten years old. Yet some of the assumptions of the founding fathers were already eroding. They had hoped to prevent the emergence of political factions, but differences over policies had produced two parties that were deeply suspicious of each other. With the retirement of George Washington, the Federalists were in decline. The new president, John Adams, had narrowly defeated Thomas Jefferson, the leader of the Democratic-Republicans.

At this moment, when the country's democratic institutions were new and fragile, the possibility of war with France loomed, and the nation was unprepared for a conflict with a major power. Moreover, there were no precedents for handling dissent. The First Amendment promised Americans freedom of speech and freedom of the press, but the language of the Constitution did not clearly delineate the extent of these freedoms.

Matthew Lyon was the first victim during the age of martyrs. The American government would censor a wide variety of speech for more than a century, and many men and women who would fight for free expression rights would suffer dire consequences.

Lyon had fought in the Battle of Saratoga, which blocked the advance of British troops marching south from Canada. The victory was crucial because it convinced France to enter the war on the side of the Americans.

But the good feelings between the Americans and the French began to wane as France experienced its own revolution that started as an effort to reform the monarchy and quickly led to a reign of terror that cost the lives of the king, his family, and tens of thousands of aristocrats.

The developments in France were deeply shocking to the ruling classes in Europe and Britain, who mobilized military forces in an effort to prevent the spread of the revolutionary contagion to their countries. In the United States, the Federalists shared this fear, and the relationship between the former allies became increasingly strained after France declared war on Britain.

Even after learning of the executions, however, many Americans continued to feel strong bonds of sympathy with the French. They saw in the struggle against a despotic ruler a replay of their own fight against King George and welcomed the revolution as confirmation that democracy would eventually conquer the world.

"This is a day of general insurrection of Man against their tyrants and cruel usurpers of their rights," Lyon wrote in the *Farmers' Library*, a newspaper he founded to expound his political views. "A day when every Despot from the great Moguls of Emperors of the East, down to the Kings and petty princes of Europe. . . . are trembling for fear of the loss of that power they have so cabbalistically [*sic*] acquired over Man."[3]

Tensions were growing. Although the Adams administration sought to remain neutral in the war between France and Britain, the French accused it of siding with their enemy. When Adams sent emissaries to negotiate, they were met with a demand that they pay a large bribe first.

Americans were outraged. Many Federalists demanded an immediate declaration of war. They also saw this as a moment to attack Lyon and other leaders of the emerging Democratic-Republican Party. "I believe there are men in this country, in this House [of Representatives], whose hatred and abhorrence of our Government lead them to prefer another, profligate and ferocious as it is," one Federalist declared.[4] The accusation that those who disagree with conservatives must hate America has been made repeatedly throughout our nation's history and continues to be made in the present day.

The Federalists and the Republicans disagreed about more than foreign policy. They held fundamentally different views of the political process itself. Federalists rejected the idea of opposing political parties altogether. It was their view that once voters had elected the nation's leaders, they were obliged to support the government's policies. So, at a time when the country faced the threat of war, they saw nothing wrong with passing a law that banned criticism of the president and Congress.

On July 4, 1798, Congress enacted a Sedition Act that punished with imprisonment and a heavy fine anyone who wrote, published, or spoke anything "false, scandalous or malicious" about federal officials in an effort to "excite against them the hatred of the people."[5]

Republicans had a different opinion. They had organized to represent people who opposed the Federalists, and they believed they had a legitimate role to play as critics of the government. They argued that the Sedition Act violated the Constitution. Jefferson, who was the leader of the Democratic-Republicans and had lost the presidential election of 1796 to Adams, expressed his outrage to James Madison. "They have brought into the lower house a sedition bill which among other enormities, undertakes to make printing certain matters criminal tho' one of the amendments of the Constitution has so expressly taken religion, printing press, etc. out of their coercion," he wrote.[6]

Lyon, who had joined his Republican colleagues in denouncing the Sedition Act on the floor of the House, was in no doubt about the effect of this, the first violation of the First Amendment. He warned that if the bill became law, people "had better hold their tongues and make toothpicks of their pens."[7]

Lyon was also aware of the personal consequences of the legislation. "[I]t was doubtlessly intended for members of Congress, and very likely would be brought to bear on me the very first," he wrote to another House member. On October 5, a friend appeared at the door of his home in Vermont to warn that a grand jury made up of his political enemies was about to indict him under the Sedition

Act. He rejected the suggestion that he flee and quietly submitted to arrest the following night.[8]

Lyon's trial started four days later before two Federalist judges. He stood accused of violating the law by writing a letter to the editor of a local newspaper that described the Adams administration as "swallowed up in a continual grasp for power, in an unbounded thirst for ridiculous pomp, foolish adulation or selfish avarice." Two additional charges in the indictment involved the publication in his own newspaper of a letter by someone else that was highly critical of the government.[9]

There was little doubt that Lyon would be convicted. He didn't deny writing the letter or publishing the other criticism. The only substantive issue was whether he intended to defame Adams. Acting as his own lawyer, Lyon attempted to prove the truth of his claims, even calling to the stand the presiding judge, William Paterson, in an effort to establish that he had seen evidence of Adams's "ridiculous pomp and parade" while dining with the president. Paterson denied it and later gave instructions to the jury that virtually guaranteed a conviction.

Lyon was not surprised when he was found guilty and fined $1,000, but he was shocked when Paterson sentenced him to four months in prison. A marshal who was one of his political enemies immediately took custody and displayed him to jubilant Federalists during a circuitous two-day journey to jail. Lyon was imprisoned in a bitterly cold cell many miles from his family. In the corner sat a bucket that Lyon said emitted "a stench about equal to the Philadelphia docks in the month of August."[10]

Over the next two years, the Federalists used the Sedition Act to charge 126 of their critics. Jefferson called it "the reign of witches." "No person who was not a witness of the scenes of that gloomy period, can form any idea of the afflicting persecutions and personal indignities that we had to brook," he said.[11]

While some of the victims were ordinary citizens like Luther

Baldwin, who drunkenly shouted that Adams was "a damned rascal and ought to have his arse kicked," the real goal of the Federalists was to secure the reelection of Adams in 1800, when he would again face Jefferson. They prosecuted the editors of four of the five major Republican newspapers. One was sentenced to six months in prison for publishing a mild criticism of the president; another received nine months for writing that the "reign of Mr. Adams . . . has been one continued tempest of malignant passions."[12]

The repression backfired. While Lyon was still in prison, the Kentucky and Virginia legislatures passed resolutions drafted by Jefferson and James Madison that declared the Sedition Act violated the First Amendment. Republicans and even moderate Federalists were outraged that the government was punishing men for their beliefs. "Men's opinions are as various as their faces, and the truth or falseness of these opinions are not fit subjects for the decision of a jury," a Republican congressman observed.[13]

The first sign of strong popular disapproval of the Sedition Act came in the form of Lyon's resounding victory in his bid for reelection from his jail cell. On his release, he was greeted by a large crowd of supporters who accompanied him for miles as he began his journey back to Congress.

He was hailed as a hero at every stop. He was a major attraction during the national campaign leading to the 1800 elections, touring the South and spending more than a month making speeches in Virginia. "Being just out of prison, I was looked to as a martyr, and every word had weight," he said.[14]

The Republicans triumphed, electing Jefferson and taking control of the House.

The Sedition Act expired on the last day of the Adams administration in 1801. Prior to its passage, most Americans had not appreciated the importance of the First Amendment. When it was written, "few of us [had] any distinct Ideas of its Nature and Extent," Benjamin Franklin acknowledged.[15]

But the experience of seeing people imprisoned for criticizing their government drove home the fact that freedom of speech is essential to the preservation of democracy.

The new president hastened to repair the damage, pardoning everyone who had been convicted under the law and ordering the immediate release of those who were still in prison. Forty years later, Congress would pay reparations to the heirs of the victims.

Today the repudiation of the Sedition Act is seen as a landmark in establishing American freedom. In 1964, the Supreme Court reaffirmed the "profound national commitment to the principle that debate on public issues should be uninhibited, robust and wide open. . . . [T]his is the lesson to be drawn from the great controversy over the Sedition Act of 1798."[16]

A Very Precious Right

In 1801, democracy in the United States was skin-deep. With few exceptions, only adult white men could vote, and not even all of them. Ten of the sixteen states limited voting to men who held enough property or other wealth to demonstrate that they had a stake in the running of the government. Catholics could not vote in five states, and Jews were barred in four.

As a result, it is estimated that 30 to 40 percent of white males were disenfranchised. Most property restrictions were soon dropped, but the country's one million women were still denied the right to vote. Extending the right to vote to Blacks and Native Americans was inconceivable. The nation had a population of nearly one million Black men and women; nine hundred thousand were slaves.

The fact that women and people of color could not vote did not mean they were powerless. From the beginning, they fought for their rights.

On a cold winter day in January 1817, free Blacks gathered in a Philadelphia church to express their outrage over an organized

Member certificate of the American Colonization Society

effort to send them to Africa. Black Americans had every reason to be suspicious of the motives of the newly formed American Colonization Society (ACS). While some supporters of colonization may have been motivated by humanitarian concerns, it was clear that most white Americans saw colonization as a way to purge the country of people they considered inferior.

Philadelphia contained the largest free Black population in the country — twenty-two thousand — and no fewer than three thousand managed to cram into the Bethel church, representing every element of the Black community. James Forten, a wealthy businessman, addressed the crowd. Behind him sat leaders of the African Methodist Episcopal Church and the African Presbyterian Church. Most of the audience was made up of men and women who lived on the margins of white society and were engaged in the dirtiest jobs for the lowest pay.

Advocates for the colonization scheme, almost all of them white, argued that Blacks had a better chance for success in Africa.

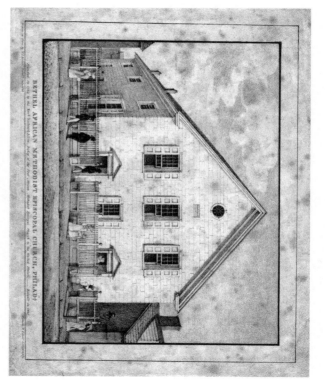

Bethel African Methodist Episcopal Church, Philadelphia, by William Breton, 1829

Forten asked for the ayes of those who believed in the premise. Dead silence. He then called on those who opposed. Every voice responded with a no that was so loud and long that it "seemed as it would bring down the walls of the building," Forten wrote.[17]

Blacks deeply resented the idea that their presence in America was a problem. "We are *natives* of this country," the Reverend Peter Williams said on the Fourth of July. "Not a few of our fathers suffered and bled to purchase its independence; we ask only to be treated as well as those who fought against it." A Black woman, Maria W. Stewart, one of the first American-born women to speak in public, excoriated the ACS in one of her earliest speeches. She swore that she would never accept exile, even if "the bayonet will pierce me through."[18]

Black resistance to colonization grew in the following years. There were more protest meetings in Philadelphia. When a Black group in Baltimore mildly endorsed the ACS in 1826, the Philadelphians held another mass meeting and issued a formal statement accusing it of misrepresenting their race.

Protests forced a Black editor who had endorsed colonization to resign from the newspaper that he founded. He complained of the "violent persecution" that he had suffered at the hands of "the most influential of our people." In the early 1830s, protest meetings were held in twenty-two cities.[19]

The anger of free Blacks found a powerful voice in David Walker. His father was a slave who died before his birth. His mother, who was free, raised him in Wilmington, North Carolina. As a young man, he moved to Charleston, South Carolina, where he found an active community of free Blacks and joined the African Methodist Episcopal Church, the first Black church in America. He finally settled in Boston in the mid-1820s and opened a store that sold new and used clothing.

Walker actively opposed slavery as a member of Prince Hall Freemasonry, a Black fraternity, and later helped found the Massachusetts General Colored Association. He was also the Boston sales agent for *The Rights of All*, the successor to America's first Black newspaper.

Walker gained a reputation as a lay preacher who knew how to use the compelling rhythms of the Methodist pulpit. In 1829, he used that knowledge to write a searing condemnation of slavery, *Walker's Appeal . . . to the Colored Citizens of the World*. In its seventy-six pages, the *Appeal* attacked the barbarity of slaveholders, the failure of the Christian churches to condemn slavery, and the colonization schemes that insulted Black Americans.

Walker also lambasted free Blacks for their servility in the presence of whites and urged them to inspire anger in their sons by giving them Thomas Jefferson's *Notes on Virginia* with its racist assumptions about Black inferiority. But he directed the *Appeal* mainly to "whites," a term he used interchangeably with "Americans."

"Remember Americans, that we must and shall be free and enlightened as you are. . . ." Walker wrote. "[W]ill you wait until we shall, under God, obtain our liberty by the crushing arm of power? Will it not be dreadful for you? I speak Americans for your own good."[20]

Walker's Appeal was deeply shocking to white America. Even those who favored abolition of slavery believed it was too extreme. People in slaveholding states condemned it as a call for enslaved people to rise against their masters, something they had done not long before in Haiti. Southern officials tried to suppress the publication. Four Black men were arrested in New Orleans with Walker's pamphlet in their possession. Thirty copies were discovered in the free Black section of Richmond, Virginia.

Anticipating the crackdown, Walker sewed his pamphlet into the clothing of Black sailors, but they were barred from disembarking in Savannah, Georgia. State legislatures considered new restrictions on "the circulation of pamphlets of evil tendency among our domestics." One bill proposed to make its circulation punishable by death.[21]

Walker was the first Black man in the United States to openly and widely express the rage of members of his race to white Americans. He died in the midst of the controversy he had created — but not before his words had pierced the consciences of some who would soon echo the demand for an immediate end to slavery. Just a few months after the publication of *Walker's Appeal*, a young, beardless editor in Boston issued the first copy of *The Liberator*, the newspaper that would launch a national abolitionist movement.

William Lloyd Garrison had been advocating for an end to slavery for several years. He had already been imprisoned for his efforts. While editing another paper, Garrison had called attention to the involvement of a prominent shipper in the slave trade. The shipper sued for libel. What Garrison said was true, but at the time the truth was not an absolute defense. The shipper needed only to prove that his reputation had been damaged. Garrison was fined $50. When he refused to pay, he was sentenced to six months in jail. He was released after seven weeks when an admirer paid his fine.

Garrison was a deeply religious man with a God-given mission. "It is my shame that I have done so little for people of color," he wrote in the Baltimore jail. "I am willing to be persecuted, imprisoned and bound for advocating African rights, and I should deserve to be a slave myself, if I shrunk from that duty or danger."[22]

In the months after his release, he sought financial support for a newspaper that would take up Walker's call for the immediate abolition of slavery. Not surprisingly, he found it in the Black community in Boston. During a meeting with its leading men and women, he promised that his newspaper would help them fight for respect, their rights as citizens, better education for their children, and an end to slavery. They agreed to help him raise money, and a committee of women was formed to join the effort. James Forten, the Philadelphia businessman, paid for the paper that was used to print the first issue of *The Liberator*.

Garrison delivered on his promise to be bold. In his inaugural issue, he broke decisively with those who were advocating colonization as the way to end slavery. He rejected the "doctrine of gradual abolition" and promised to "strenuously contend for the immediate enfranchisement of our slave population."[23]

He also swore to fight slaveholders with everything in his power. "I will be as harsh as truth and as uncompromising as justice," he wrote. "On this subject I do not wish to think or speak, or write, with moderation. No! No! . . . I am in earnest — I will not equivocate — I will not excuse — I will not retreat a single inch — AND I WILL BE HEARD!"[24]

The young editor was soon given an opportunity to prove his courage. Eight months after the launch of *The Liberator*, in August 1831, Nat Turner, a slave, led a bloody uprising in Virginia that resulted in the deaths of seventy whites, including women and children. As a pacifist, Garrison could not condone the rebellion, but he also refused to condemn it. "In his fury against the revolters, who will remember their wrongs?" he asked.[25]

Garrison's newspaper was accused, without evidence, of helping foment the insurrection. Georgetown, a part of the District of Columbia, passed an ordinance that prohibited free Blacks from retrieving copies of *The Liberator* from the post office under the penalty of a fine, and violators who could not pay the fine would be sold into slavery.

A grand jury in Raleigh, North Carolina, indicted Garrison for distributing incendiary material. The editor laughed at the offer of a $1,500 reward in South Carolina for the conviction of any white person who distributed his paper. "[W]e think we are worth more," he joked. But he was outraged when the Georgia legislature offered $5,000 to anyone who could capture him and bring him south to face trial for libel. He denounced it as "a bribe to kidnappers."[26]

Yet with every word of condemnation and every threat of arrest, the defenders of slavery brought more attention to Garrison and his cause. Convinced that the goal of emancipation depended on building a national organization, Garrison called an organizational meeting in Philadelphia in December 1833.

At first, the attendees were unable to find a place to meet. Public halls and churches refused to host them. But the Black community welcomed them, and they met in a small building adjacent to the city's oldest Black church. Delegates from out of town stayed with Black families.

Following several days of meetings, the abolitionists launched the American Anti-Slavery Society (AASS), which pledged to organize groups "in every city, town and village of our land," hire recruiting agents, circulate anti-slavery tracts, and enlist the press in the campaign to "remove slavery by moral and political action." They saw their task as fulfilling the promises of the Declaration of Independence and held a formal ceremony during which each of the sixty-three delegates came forward to sign a document inscribed on parchment.[27]

The AASS launched its first assault on the institution of slavery through the mail. Garrison had long anticipated a campaign that would "scatter tracts like raindrops, over the land, filled with startling facts and melting appeals on the subject of Negro oppression. . . ."[28]

In May 1835, the AASS approved a plan that was more analogous to a flood. Recent inventions had revolutionized the printing process, making it possible to lower the cost and increase the speed of publishing. The AASS began printing twenty to fifty thousand copies per week of publications with titles like *Human Rights, The Anti-Slavery Record,* and *The Emancipator. The Slave's Friend* was written for children. There were also woodcuts, etchings, kerchiefs, and even chocolate wrappers.

The AASS distributed more than one million pieces during the first year, sending the abolitionist message into every corner of the rapidly expanding country. This was particularly important for getting material to opinion leaders in the South, where it was too dangerous for its agents to travel.

It did not take long before Southerners complained that they were under attack. In July, alerted by rumors that packages of "incendiary" material had arrived on a mail steamer in Charleston, South Carolina, men broke into the United States post office. They seized the offending publications and burned them as a crowd of three thousand watched. Effigies of Garrison and Arthur Tappan, another prominent abolitionist, were hung nearby.

Local committees formed throughout the South to censor the mails and watch for abolitionists. In Nashville, Tennessee, a traveling evangelist received twenty lashes in the public market after AASS pamphlets were discovered in his knapsack.

Southern politicians demanded laws that would exclude from the mails "all printed papers suspected of a tendency to produce or encourage an insubordinate and insurrectionary spirit among the slaves of the South." In a message to Congress, President Andrew Jackson expressed his support for such a ban. However, the issue became moot as postal officials throughout the South refused to deliver abolitionist literature.[29]

What worried slaveholders more than abolitionist literature in the South was the rapid growth of anti-slavery sentiment in the North. Only a fraction of the massive propaganda campaign launched by the abolitionists was mailed to slave states. The rest of the newspapers, pamphlets, and other appeals found their target, and a growing number of Americans were responding.

The American Anti-Slavery Society had 225 chapters at the beginning of its literature campaign in May 1835. The number more than doubled over the next six months and doubled again the following year.

One of the first goals of these groups was to circulate petitions demanding that Congress ban slavery from the District of Columbia, where human beings were still sold in sight of the Capitol. Soon a steady stream of petitions became a flood that threatened to drown the country's legislators.

Slavery still had many defenders in the North, however. There were important economic ties between the two regions. The cotton picked by slaves was one of the country's most important export crops and was essential to the prosperity of its major cities — New York, Philadelphia, and Boston. Abolitionists' increasingly effective efforts also provoked fear in many Americans that the end of slavery would begin an "amalgamation" through intermarriage that would raise Blacks by destroying the white race.

There was an almost immediate and violent response to the emergence of the abolitionist movement. In October 1833, a crowd of fifteen hundred in New York City surrounded a building where activists had intended to organize an anti-slavery society. The abolitionists were later chased away from a second location but not before finishing their business. There were more attacks on abolitionists in New York and Philadelphia the following summer. Mobs destroyed at least sixty homes and six churches in New York.

Mob action soon spread to the rest of the country, affecting communities of every size. In most cases, the leaders of the mobs were influential citizens — "gentlemen of property and standing" — who believed it was their duty to silence the abolitionists.

If the anti-abolitionists failed to deny their enemies a place to meet, they did everything they could to disrupt them. In Circleville, Ohio, a mob used tin horns, sleigh bells, and drums to drown out the voice of abolitionist Theodore Dwight Weld as he spoke in a church. When that failed, they stoned the building, and a brick hit Weld in the head, knocking him senseless. He was able to finish his speech, but when he emerged an angry mob was waiting, armed with stones, rotten eggs, and nails, their faces blackened as a disguise.

Weld escaped unharmed, but abolitionist speakers came to expect rough handling. One authoritative source has counted 115 assaults in the 1830s and another 64 in the 1840s. Volleys of rotten eggs and vegetables were so common that speakers often wore a "storm suit" of old clothing. By the middle of 1835, Garrison was describing mob violence as a "reign of terror." A few months later, he was able to speak from personal experience.[30]

Boston's merchants had grown so worried by the threat of abolition that they held a meeting in Faneuil Hall, the scene of speeches by leaders of the American Revolution, where they announced their support for new laws that would punish the abolitionists. Within weeks, someone erected a gallows on Garrison's doorstep in the dead of night.

Tension grew as the city awaited the arrival of George Thompson, an English abolitionist. English abolitionists were hated even more than their American comrades, and a group of "patriotic citizens" issued a flyer promising a $100 reward to the first man who laid "violent hands on Thompson, so that he may be brought to the

A Boston mob attacks William Lloyd Garrison, 1835

tar-kettle before dark." On the day of the speech, five hundred copies of the flyer produced an angry crowd of several thousand.[31]

The Boston Female Anti-Slavery Society, the sponsor of the event, had already decided that it was too dangerous for Thompson to speak, but the members were determined to hold their meeting. The mob packing the street did not know that Thompson was not in the building and began shouting for him to appear.

The mayor of Boston, Theodore Lyman, attempted to restore order by announcing that Thompson was not present, but the shouting continued as two dozen members of the society started their meeting. A group of young men who had managed to enter the building added to the chaos by pounding on the door of the meeting room and throwing orange peels over the transom.

Then Lyman burst into the room with several constables and begged the women to leave, telling them that their lives were in danger. Even then, several women refused and began to argue with the mayor. At last, emerging two by two and arm in arm, the white and Black women maneuvered down the narrow path that the constables had cleared through the crowd.

Several male abolitionists remained in the building, including Garrison, who had agreed to speak in Thompson's place. The crowd began demanding the surrender of the leader of the abolitionist movement. "Out with him!" "Lynch him!" "Turn him a right nigger color with tar!"[32]

The mayor told Garrison that he could not protect him and advised him to flee out a back window. The mob had the building almost completely surrounded, but Garrison was able to get across the street, where a sympathetic carpenter tried to hide him behind some boards in his loft. The mob soon discovered Garrison and, secured with a rope that was wrapped around his chest, forced him to climb out a window and descend by ladder to the howling crowd below.

Reaching the bottom, he expected the worst, but the rope had slipped, and two muscular teamsters, Daniel and Buff Cooley, grabbed him before he could be assaulted. Although they were not abolitionists, the Cooley brothers had taken pity on Garrison, and they now rushed him forward toward city hall.

Angry men snatched at the editor, ripping his clothes and breaking his glasses, but they were unable to break the grip of the Cooleys. Garrison finally found safety in a cell of the city jail. He later fled Boston for a safe haven in Connecticut where he continued to edit his newspaper.

Physical attacks on the abolitionists declined sharply in 1836. Once they had established an anti-slavery society in a community, their opponents turned to more pressing business. However, Southerners remained deeply alarmed by the growth of abolitionism and became more determined than ever to smother criticism. Just weeks after Garrison was chased through the streets of Boston, they began to demand that members of Congress stop accepting petitions calling for an end to slavery.

Such petitions were nothing new. When they were arrived, they were opened and then routinely tabled and received no further consideration. However, the rise of abolitionism placed the petitions in a new light. They called on Congress to ban slavery in the District of Columbia and take other steps that would lead to its abolition.

Southerners rejected any suggestion that the federal government could regulate slavery, and they demanded that such appeals be silenced. "I cannot see the rights of the Southern people assaulted day after day, by the ignorant fanatics from whom these memorials proceed," a congressman from South Carolina exclaimed during a House debate.[33]

Once again Northerners rallied in support of slavery. The House of Representatives overwhelmingly approved resolutions that denied that Congress possessed the power to ban slavery in any state or the District of Columbia. It also declared that "all petitions, memorials, resolutions, propositions, papers relating in any way or to any extent whatever to the subject of slavery or the abolition of slavery shall, without being printed or referred, be laid upon the table and that no further action whatever be taken thereon."[34]

The House had imposed a gag rule on its members and violated an essential freedom of democracy — the right to petition the government. But one member of the House rose to declare that he would not be gagged.

At sixty-eight, John Quincy Adams was an old man for his time. He was also the most distinguished member of Congress. The son of President John Adams, he had served as secretary of state, an ambassador, a member of the Senate, and the sixth president of the United States. Although not an abolitionist, he would spend the next five years in a lonely fight "to sustain the right of petition in the citizen, and the freedom of thought in this House, and the freedom of the press, and of thought, out of it."[35]

His opponents tried everything they could to shut up Adams, and the gag rule gave them the power to table every effort he made to take action on an abolitionist petition. But the old man was a master of parliamentary procedure. In 1837, soon after the gag rule had been reauthorized, he used a ruse to get the House to discuss two petitions that he had received.

One was from nine free Black women in Virginia. The representative from that district rose to say one of the women was a prostitute. Adams asked how he knew the women were "infamous," and the Virginian answered that he only knew one of them. Adams acknowledged the clarification. "I might have asked him who it was that made these women infamous — whether it was those of their own color or their masters," Adams said. This reference to the well-known but unacknowledged fact that slave owners raped their servants caused "great sensation," according to the House scribe.[36]

Then Adams turned to the second petition, which purported to be from slaves. No one had ever attempted to introduce such a petition. When he revealed that the petition actually supported slavery and was therefore coerced, the House exploded with calls to punish Adams. There were "loud cries of 'he ought to be expelled'" and "Cries of 'no!' 'no!' Expel him! Expel the mover!'"[37]

A Georgia representative called for a public burning of the petition. The House spent days considering a motion to censure Adams, but it was unable to bring itself to humiliate a former president.

At the start of the controversy over the gag rule, Adams had warned Southerners that they were handing the abolitionists an excellent opportunity to build support. Now the American Anti-Slavery Society began to organize a national campaign, using their powerful printing presses in New York to send blank petitions to more than a thousand local societies. The forms began to appear in stores and churches and at county fairs. Most were carried from door to door. The petitions began to flood both the House and Senate. Hundreds of thousands petitions arrived in the first eighteen months of the campaign.

The AASS estimated that more than two million people signed the petitions during 1838 and 1839. This was especially alarming to pro-slavery Southerners and their supporters, because the abolitionists only numbered around one hundred thousand at the time. Clearly, many Americans who were not openly abolitionists were sympathetic to the plight of enslaved people and might one day support the end of slavery.

But many people who signed the petitions were motivated by a desire to protect free expression rights; namely, the right to petition and also freedom of the press. Pro-slavery Southerners had been urging suppression of the abolitionist press for years. In early 1836, legislatures in the slave states formally asked the Northern states to pass censorship laws. The debate over these requests was under way when the citizens of Cincinnati took matters into their own hands.

A gang of twenty men, including several prominent business owners, broke into the offices of a printer who was publishing a new abolitionist newspaper, *Philanthropist*. They tore up the forms that contained the next issue of the paper and then dismantled the press itself, taking away all the pieces they could carry.

The Ohio Anti-Slavery Society announced its intention to continue publishing *Philanthropist*. "We have embraced with a full determination by the help of God to maintain unimpaired the freedom of speech and the liberty of the press, *the palladium of our rights*," it declared. During two days of rioting that included attacks on the Black section of town, a mob attacked the printer again, and this time destroyed his press.[38]

Newspapers throughout the North generally scorned the abolitionists, but they were quick to condemn the violent attack on press freedom. "We hold that this combination of the few to govern the many by terror of illegal violence is as wicked and indefensible as a conspiracy to rob on the highway," the *New-York Evening Post* declared.[39]

There was worse to come. In the same month as the Cincinnati riots, a young editor named Elijah P. Lovejoy was forced to flee St. Louis. Lovejoy was not an abolitionist. A Presbyterian minister, he had taken charge of a religious newspaper, the *Observer*, which spent more time condemning Catholics than slavery.

Yet his support for gradual emancipation in Missouri, a slave state, prompted demands for suppression. A meeting of citizens sent him a warning. "Freedom of speech and press does not imply a moral right . . . to freely discuss the subject of slavery," it said, ". . . a question too nearly allied the vital interests of the slaveholding States to admit of public disputation."[40]

Lovejoy refused to quit. When he condemned the torture and murder of a Black man accused of killing a policeman, a mob attacked his office and damaged his press. Fearing for the safety of his young family, he decided to move to Illinois, where he believed he would be free to express his views. He was mistaken. Although he had crossed the Mississippi River into a free state, Alton was only thirty miles north of St. Louis, and its leading citizens were just as worried about abolitionism as the people in Missouri.

Lovejoy soon faced strong pressure from large public meetings. But he remained stubbornly committed to his anti-slavery views. Over the next year and a half, vandals attacked his press three times. With a small group of supporters, Lovejoy was determined to defend the fourth press. He secretly moved it to a brick warehouse where he thought he could protect it. But an armed mob surrounded the building, and there was an exchange of gunfire. Lovejoy was hit several times and killed.

When the men inside the warehouse surrendered, members of the mob entered. Not satisfied with the death of the editor, they destroyed the press and threw its pieces in the Mississippi River.

Elijah Lovejoy died defending freedom of the press. His death shocked the nation. Southern editors joined those in the North in condemning the action of the mob as a fundamental violation

Siege of the brick warehouse where Elijah P. Lovejoy hid his fourth printing press and was murdered, 1837

of American liberty. In Boston, where a mob had nearly lynched Garrison two years earlier, Faneuil Hall, the Cradle of Liberty, was the site of the nation's largest protest meeting.

Not everyone in attendance viewed Lovejoy as a hero. James T. Austin, the attorney general of the state, blamed abolitionists for frightening the South with the specter of freeing "wild beasts." He called the members of the mob patriots like those who threw tea into the harbor during the Boston Tea Party. Lovejoy got what he deserved and "died as the fool dieth," Austin said.[41]

Wendell Phillips, a twenty-six-year-old attorney from one of the city's best families, rose to respond. He said he was stunned that Austin compared the Alton mob to the leaders of the American Revolution. He had expected "the earth to have yawned and swallowed him up." Many years later, Phillips would say that Lovejoy's death "stunned a drunken people into sobriety." "The gun fired at Lovejoy was like that of [Fort] Sumter — it shattered a world of dreams."[42]

However, the firing on Fort Sumter that began the Civil War was still two decades in the future. The abolitionists remained a negligible force, and they continued to search for every opportunity to draw attention to their cause.

Four years after Lovejoy's death, they discovered Frederick Douglass, who would become one of the great figures of his time. Douglass escaped from slavery in 1838 at the age of twenty. By that time, he had suffered many deprivations and cruelties, including separation from his mother when he was six, many beatings, and a failed escape attempt.

He had also learned to read and had led a Sabbath school for slaves from neighboring plantations until it was broken up by angry whites. After settling in New Bedford, Massachusetts, which was home to a large Black community, Douglass worked as a day laborer and was soon licensed as a preacher by the African Methodist Episcopal Zion Church.

His first speech was an attack on colonization that he delivered to a Black audience. After several more speeches at an abolitionist convention in 1841, Garrison hired him as a lecturer, and he began an extensive speaking tour of New England and New York.

Abolitionist audiences were hungry to hear the stories of escaped slaves. Although Douglass was only one of several who were touring, he quickly became the star. He was a gifted public speaker who knew how to grab an audience. "I appear before the immense assembly this evening as a thief and a robber," he said at the beginning of an early speech. "I stole this head, these limbs, this body from my master and ran off with them."[43]

He had a lively sense of humor, which he used to mock the myth of Black inferiority. His compelling personal story melted the hearts of listeners. But he also possessed a deep anger that he unleashed to flay slaveholders and their defenders, saving special fury for the ministers who used the Bible to justify the evil of owning human beings.

Several years after he took to the road, Douglass published a memoir, *Narrative of the Life of Frederick Douglass, An American Slave*, which became a bestseller on two continents. He soon embarked on a European tour. On his return, he founded a newspaper, *The North Star*, which gave him a national vehicle for his views.

Douglass was a target wherever he went. He and his party were assaulted several times with stones and rotten eggs when they arrived in Pendleton, Indiana, where he was scheduled to deliver a speech. Many Southerners had settled in Indiana, and a hostile crowd of drunken men blocked the entrance to the church where Douglass and his companions were to speak. They pushed through the crowd without incident the first night. But the church shut its doors to them the following day.

When the abolitionists gathered 130 followers for an open-air meeting, a mob led by man in a coonskin cap surrounded them. A few men attacked the speakers' platform, setting off a riot. Douglass tried to fight back. Amid cries of "kill the nigger," he was clubbed "prostrate on the ground under a torrent of blows . . . my right hand broken, and in a state of unconsciousness," he recalled. [44]

Only quick action by a fellow abolitionist who tackled the assailant saved Douglass from further injury. He was carried by a wagon to a friendly home where he recovered enough to speak again the following night. For the rest of his life he wrote with a hand that never regained its full strength and dexterity.

Douglass had to fight for the right to be heard often during the following years. In 1854, he was involved in a controversy with Illinois senator Stephen A. Douglas, the author of a law that left the status of slavery in the Kansas Territory up to the settlers, prompting a violent conflict between pro-slavery and free-soil factions. When Frederick Douglass announced that he would speak in Chicago, the senator's supporters condemned his impudence for presuming to speak on his opponent's home turf.

As he began his speech, he paused to address the charge. "I am not ashamed of being called an intruder. I have met it a thousand times in a thousand different places. Every inch of ground occupied by the colored man in this country is sternly disputed," he said. [45]

FIGHTING THE MOB IN INDIANA.

Violence at an abolitionist gathering in Indiana featuring Frederick Douglass, 1843

"I have a right to be here and a duty to perform here. That right is a constitutional right as well as a natural right." It was a right denied to three million slaves, Douglass said. "[T]hey are dumb in their chains! . . . There are special reasons, therefore, why I should speak and speak freely. The right of speech is a very precious one, especially to the oppressed."[46]

Six years later, Douglass was the victim of another mob in Boston. It was December 1860, a month after Abraham Lincoln was elected president. Southerners had made it clear that they would not accept a president who was anti-slavery, and South Carolina was preparing to be the first state to secede.

Panicked Northerners blamed the abolitionists for leading the country to the brink of civil war. There were violent attacks on them in several Northern cities. Douglass was scheduled to speak at a meeting commemorating the anniversary of the death of John Brown, the abolitionist martyr.

But many men in the audience were there to disrupt the meeting. After hours of shouting, fighting erupted. Once again, Douglass was at the center of the melee, attempting to repel invaders to the stage. Finally, the police, who had refused to provide protection for the meeting, restored peace by expelling everyone from the building.

Several days later, Douglass talked again about the importance of free speech. Addressing another audience, he expressed surprise at encountering so much resistance in Boston. "The mortifying and disgraceful fact stares us in the face, that though Faneuil Hall and Bunker Hill Monument stand, freedom of speech is struck down," he said. "Not even an old-fashioned abolition meeting could vindicate that right in Boston just now."[47]

Douglass observed that some were saying the organizers of the meeting were as much to blame as the rioters. "What is the matter with us?" he asked. "After all the arguments for liberty to which Boston has listened for more than a quarter of a century, has she yet to learn that the time to assert a right is the time when the right itself is called into question, and that the men of all others to assert it are the men to whom the right has been denied?"

Douglass also criticized the mayor for failing to protect the meeting, pointing out that it wasn't just the speakers whose rights were violated. "To suppress free speech is a double wrong. It violates the rights of the hearer as well as those of the speaker," he said.

The Women's Movement

Blacks were not the only people fighting for their freedom. Women had launched their own liberation movement in 1848 during a convention in Seneca Falls, New York.

White women certainly enjoyed a social position that was far superior to any slave. Men honored them as wives and mothers. But they were expected to confine themselves to domestic concerns because they were not believed to be strong enough or smart enough to contend in the world of men.

No woman made a public speech in the United States until Frances Wright, a Scottish radical, toured the country in 1828. The first American woman to make a speech may have been Maria Stewart, the Black woman who first raised her voice against the American Colonization Society. She spoke against slavery in Boston for several years in the early 1830s but soon abandoned the experiment. "I have made myself contemptible in the eyes of many," she explained.[48]

Women faced many legal restrictions as well as prejudice. While single women possessed many of the same rights as men, married women had none. A man took control of whatever property a woman brought into their marriage. Husbands were the masters of their wives.

Yet, very slowly at first, women were making progress. They sought expanded educational opportunities, and once they had secured them, many became teachers and helped other women broaden their horizons.

The fight against slavery provided entry into the political world for many women. In the largest cities, they formed their own abolitionist groups. The Boston Female Anti-Slavery Society organized the meeting that was the occasion for the anti-Garrison riot in Boston. Because male abolitionists were busy earning a living, women provided much of the energy that drove the national petition campaign. "My husband and I are busy in that most odious of all tasks, that of getting signatures to petitions," Lydia Maria Child, a popular writer, explained in a letter.[49]

Carrying petitions from door to door was exhausting work. It also took a lot of courage for a housewife, mother, or daughter to set off unaccompanied by a man and walk down unfamiliar streets where they were often met with hostility for acting in such an "unwomanly matter." Historical archives contain thousands of yellowed petitions that are proof of their determination.

Then women began to speak out publicly against slavery. Several years after Maria Stewart had abandoned her talks, abolitionist friends urged Sarah and Angelina Grimke to begin telling the story of why they had fled from their slaveholding family in South Carolina. They planned to start with a small gathering in someone's home, but there was so much interest that the meeting was moved to a small church. More than three hundred women showed up.

At the next meeting, a man appeared but was turned away from the women-only event. As the popularity of the Grimkes grew, more men wanted to attend their meetings, and in short order the Grimkes were addressing large mixed audiences.

There was a public backlash against the Grimkes and other women who were active in the abolitionist movement. In the House of Representatives, Benjamin C. Howard, a representative from Maryland, bemoaned the fact that so many of the petitions that were flooding the Capitol were coming from women.

According to a summary of Howard's remarks, "[H]e thought that these females could have a sufficient field for the exercise of their influence in the discharge of their duties to their fathers, their husbands or their children."[50]

John Quincy Adams, whose mother, Abigail, had argued for giving the vote to women, responded in a long speech detailing the achievements of heroic women throughout the ages and during the American Revolution. He concluded by inviting any colleague to communicate his concerns directly to the Grimkes. "And if he does enter on the discussion, all I shall say is that I wish him well out of it," Adams said, prompting laughter.[51]

But the criticism heaped on the Grimkes was not a laughing matter. Without naming them, the Council of Congregationalist Ministers of Massachusetts issued a pastoral letter condemning their activism. "[W]hen [a woman] assumes the place and tone of man as a public reformer . . . her character becomes unnatural," it said.[52]

Such efforts to disapprove and intimidate did not stop Angelina from addressing a committee of the Massachusetts legislature, the first time a woman had appeared before a legislative body. However, it took all her strength to do so. "I was so near fainting under the tremendous pressure of feeling, my heart almost died within me," she wrote. "The novelty of the scene, the weight of responsibility, the ceaseless exercise of mind thro' which I passed for almost a week — all together sunk me to the earth . . . [M]y limbs trembling beneath me, I stood up and spoke for nearly two hours." Several months later, Angelina suffered a breakdown and did not give another speech for many years.[53]

Sarah Grimke fired back at critics. "To me it is perfectly clear that whatsoever it is morally right for a man to do, it is morally right for a woman to do," she wrote.[54]

This was too radical for many abolitionists. Even Theodore Weld, who would marry Angelina, urged the sisters to drop the women's rights issue because it would alienate support for abolition. Other male abolitionists rejected the idea of female equality altogether.

In 1840, there was a heated debate at the World Anti-Slavery Convention in London over whether to allow women in the American delegation to serve as delegates. The women lost, prompting two of them, Lucretia Mott and Elizabeth Cady Stanton, to begin discussing the idea of a campaign for women's rights.

Eight years later, three hundred men and women gathered at

A *Harper's Weekly* cartoon parodying the 1848 women's rights convention in Seneca Falls, suggesting that suffrage is contrary to religious and natural law

Seneca Falls in upstate New York to lay the groundwork of the women's movement.

Things got off to a rough start when the attendees discovered locked doors at the church where they were to meet. They boosted someone through a window, and the proceeding got under way. None of the women felt qualified to serve as chair, so Mott's husband assumed the role.

There was little disagreement over a proposed "Declaration of Sentiments" that called for social, civil, and religious equality for women. However, Stanton had included a demand that women have the right to vote. When she read a draft to her husband, he told her he would leave town if she insisted on the vote. She did — and he did.

Even Lucretia Mott opposed Stanton, fearing that opposition to empowering women with the right to vote would make it harder to achieve their other goals. But Frederick Douglass, the only Black person at the meeting, strongly supported Stanton and helped turn opinion in her favor. He was one of thirty-two men who joined sixty-eight women in signing the declaration.

The leaders of the new women's movement knew that they would face enormous resistance. "In entering upon the great work before us, we anticipate no small amount of misconception, misrepresentation, and ridicule," they wrote. But they expressed confidence in the tools that were available to them. "We shall employ agents, circulate tracts, petition the State and national legislatures, and endeavor to enlist the pulpit and press on our behalf."⁵⁵

Above all, they drew strength from the enthusiasm of other women. "We find that many of our New England sisters are prepared to receive these strange doctrines, feeling as they do that our whole sex needs emancipation," Angelina Grimke wrote to a friend. "What dost thou think of them *walking* two, four, six and eight miles to attend our meetings?"⁵⁶

They were right about the ridicule. Hecklers were disrupting a women's rights convention in Akron, Ohio, until Sojourner Truth advanced to the stage. Truth was a well-known abolitionist who had been a slave in upstate New York until the state legislature abolished slavery in 1827. Her master had forced her to marry against her will, and most of her thirteen children were sold into slavery.

The hecklers hissed her as she laid her bonnet at her feet and turned to address them. She was following a minister who had delivered an insulting speech about the weakness of women.

Truth raised her muscled arm. "Look at my arm," she demanded. "I have ploughed and planted and gathered into barns, and no man could head me — and ain't I a woman? I could work as much and eat as much as a man — when I could get it — and bear the lash as well. And ain't I a woman?"⁵⁷

The women in the audience went wild. "Amid roars of applause she returned to her corner, leaving more than one of us with streaming eyes, and hearts beating with gratitude," Frances Dana

Gage, the meeting chairperson, recalled. "She had taken us up in her strong arms . . . turning the whole tide in our favor."[58]

Susan B. Anthony, another strong woman, became the movement's master tactician. In her first campaign, she launched a petition drive to support a women's rights bill in the New York legislature, appointing captains to direct the drive in the state's sixty counties.

"Like itinerant tin pedlars [sic] or book agents they tramped the streets and country roads, knocking at every door, presenting their petitions, arguing with women who half the time slammed the door in their faces with the smug remark that they had husbands, thank God, to look after their interests," Anthony recalled.[59]

In ten weeks, they collected six thousand signatures and won a hearing for their bill. When the bill didn't pass, Anthony embarked on a speaking tour in the dead of winter in 1855, visiting fifty-six counties. Five years later the bill became law.

Anthony excelled at getting publicity. In 1872, she was arrested for voting in the presidential election. In 1876, during the first World's Fair held in the United States, she and four other women appeared uninvited on the main stage and handed the startled chairman a parchment containing the Seneca Falls declaration.

Expecting to be arrested at any minute, they exited through the audience, distributing flyers from their large handbags as they went. Outside they captured an empty bandstand. In the hot sun, one of the women held an umbrella over Anthony's head as she read the declaration to a large crowd.

Despite the hard work and daring of the activists, progress in the fight for women's rights was slow. There were many obstacles in their path, including the federal government.

In 1873, Congress passed a national censorship law, the Comstock Act. Anthony Comstock, the head of the New York Society for the Suppression of Vice, drafted the bill to strengthen the government's power to fight "obscenity." Comstock had been trying to suppress commercial pornography for years, and weak laws frequently frustrated his efforts. The new statute gave the federal government the power to severely punish anyone who used the mail to distribute illegal material.

Comstock, a conservative Christian, was not interested in censoring only sexually explicit books. He wanted to force everyone to abide by his definition of morality. This put him on a collision course with those who were fighting for women's rights.

One of Comstock's first targets was Victoria Woodhull. Having started her career as a spiritualist who communed with the dead, Woodhull became a national celebrity: the first female member of the New York Stock Exchange, first woman to publish a newspaper — *Woodhull and Claflin's Weekly* — and the first woman to run for president.

Her decision to publicize details of the adultery of Henry Ward Beecher, one of the country's most prominent ministers, is what attracted Comstock's attention. The article Woodhull published was not sexually explicit, but she had written about sex for a large public audience for money. According to Comstock, that made it obscene.

Woodhull was held in jail for four weeks and escaped further punishment when her case was dismissed on a technicality. But Comstock's war against people who wrote and talked about sexual matters was only getting started.

The Comstock Act had significantly expanded the definition of *obscenity*. It was now a crime to mail not just erotica but anything that promoted birth control, including contraceptive medications and devices as well as all contraception information. He used this new prohibition to go after his next victim, Dr. Edward Bliss Foote.

Foote was an active supporter of the women's rights movement. He had helped Anthony pay her fine for voting illegally and endorsed Woodhull's presidential candidacy. He was best known for his popular medical guide, which described methods of birth control. Fearing possible prosecution, he dropped these details from later publications and began sending the information in a pamphlet only to those who requested it.

Foote hoped that censoring his books would be enough, but Comstock arrested him for mailing the pamphlet. He was convicted and faced a possible ten-year prison term, but the presiding judge suspended the sentence and imposed a heavy fine. Although undoubtedly disappointed that Foote was not in jail, Comstock had achieved his goal. The suspended sentence could be imposed if Foote ever published birth control information again, and he never did.

Comstock paid special attention to the people he called "free lusters," men and women who advocated free love. They wanted to abolish all laws regulating sexual relationships. Most Americans found their views shocking, and Comstock was determined to silence them. In 1877, he attended a meeting of the New England Free Love League and listened in horror as Angela Heywood spoke about sexual intercourse to an audience of mostly men. "I could see lust in every face," he said.[60]

He rushed outside and found a policeman to arrest Angela's husband, Ezra, who was charged with distributing his pamphlet *Cupid's Yokes*. In addition to promoting free love, *Cupid's Yokes* denounced the arrest of Woodhull, called the Comstock Act a "National Gag Law," and described Comstock as "a religious monomaniac." Ezra was sentenced to two years in prison. His imprisonment outraged many liberals, who started a campaign that won his release after six months.

Comstock was relentless. He next prosecuted D. M. Bennett, the publisher of *The Truth Seeker*, a newspaper that was critical of organized religion. Bennett did not share Heywood's views on free love, but he supported his right to free speech. He was scathing in his attacks on Comstock, who arrested him three times before he finally won a conviction of Bennett for mailing *Cupid's Yokes*,

Anthony Comstock as a monk thwarting displays of excessive flesh, even by horses and dogs, by L.M. Glackens

which the editor had been selling as a symbol of his support for Heywood. He was sixty-one and in poor health when he arrived at the Albany Penitentiary, one of the nation's worst, where he served eleven months at hard labor.[61]

Meanwhile, Comstock continued his persecution of Heywood. He arrested him again, this time for publishing two poems that the publisher of Walt Whitman's *Leaves of Grass* had removed from the book after threats by a district attorney who considered them obscene. When that charge did not stick, Comstock indicted Heywood for publishing a letter that contained the word *fuck*. This time Heywood served two years.

Although Comstock and his supporters inflicted pain on many people between the passage of the Comstock Act in 1873 and his death in 1915, perhaps no one suffered more than Ida C. Craddock. Craddock was a brilliant young woman from Philadelphia who passed the entry exam at the University of Pennsylvania and would have been its first female undergraduate student if the board of trustees had not blocked her path. Undeterred, she educated herself while working as a secretary in the city's department of highways.

With a knowledge of several languages, she became a scholar of mystical religions and their sexual practices. Craddock embraced eroticism and started her own church, the Church of Yoga. She also began to counsel married couples who were having sexual problems and wrote several pamphlets that were very explicit in their advice.

Craddock's interests alarmed her mother, who had her committed briefly to an insane asylum. When Ida's employer found out about her writing, she was abruptly fired from her city job. Then police indicted her for obscenity, and she was released only after promising not to mail her pamphlets again. She moved to Chicago, which she hoped was a more liberal city.

When she was arrested again, her lawyer, Clarence Darrow, was able to get her a three-month suspended sentence in return for a guilty plea. She moved to Washington, DC, but the authorities forced her to leave. When she arrived in New York City, Comstock was waiting. He engineered her indictment on both state and federal charges. Craddock served three months in prison on the state charges. By the time she emerged, advocates of free speech were hailing her as a hero.

Her ordeal continued as Comstock pursued her conviction on the federal charges, which carried a sentence of up to ten years. Comstock was standing near her when the judge pronounced her guilty.

Craddock committed suicide before the day of her sentencing. "I am taking my life because a judge, at the instigation of Anthony Comstock, has decreed me guilty of a crime I did not commit — the circulation of obscene literature," she wrote in a letter to her lawyer.[62]

Comstock's power began to wane after the turn of the century. In 1914, the year before he died, he was still strong enough to force

Margaret Sanger to flee abroad to escape an obscenity indictment for mailing *Family Limitation*, her graphic and detailed description of birth control methods. However, public support for Sanger grew to the point where the authorities decided to drop the charges.

The growth of the women's movement was further evidence of the waning influence of Comstock's conservative values. By the first years of the twentieth century, the movement for women's suffrage had been under way for more than fifty years. In 1912, one million women were able to vote in six western states.

However, the vast majority of women remained disenfranchised. To breathe life into their campaign, the suffragists had begun to hold annual parades demanding the vote. In New York, "women who usually see Fifth Avenue through the polished windows of their limousines and touring cars strode steadily side by side with pale-faced, thin-bodied girls from the sweltering sweat shops of the East Side," a reporter wrote.[63]

The suffragists also took advantage of the invention of the automobile to carry their message quickly and easily to every community. In Massachusetts, several women generated great excitement during a "trolley tour," speaking at impromptu meetings outdoors across the state.

American activists were also watching what was happening in Great Britain, where the women's movement had taken a radical turn. Frustrated by the slow progress of the suffrage movement there, women had begun to interrupt speeches by government officials.

In 1909, Alice Paul, an American, stood up during a speech in Edinburgh by the minister of foreign affairs, who was outlining a plan for prosperity. "Well, these are wonderful ideals, but couldn't you also extend them to women?" Paul asked. The police immediately removed her from the meeting and took her to jail. The resulting publicity and outrage convinced some leaders of the campaign that they had discovered a valuable new tactic.[64]

Suffragists began to plan protests with the goal of provoking the police and generating news coverage. Some threw stones, broke windows, and even physically attacked government officials.

Although Paul was a Quaker who rejected violence, the British police arrested her several times for speaking out. When prison authorities would not grant her status as a political prisoner, she started a hunger strike, a common tactic among suffragists. Officials normally released them to avoid the negative publicity for force-feeding women prisoners.

Paul, however, was force-fed. She was tied to a chair, "then the prison doctor, assisted by two women attendants, placed a rubber tube up my nostrils and pumped liquid food through it into the stomach. Twice a day for a month . . . this was done," she recalled. Weakened by the ordeal, Paul had to be carried out of prison at the end of her sentence. Soon after, she returned to the United States and moved to Washington, DC, where she resumed her fight.[65]

Paul pursued a radical, seemingly impossible, goal. The suffrage movement had been following a strategy of winning the vote state by state, but Paul advocated for an amendment to the US Constitution that would enfranchise all women simultaneously.

She organized a suffrage parade on Pennsylvania Avenue that drew more than five thousand people on the day before the 1912 presidential inauguration. When the parade failed to convince the incoming president, Woodrow Wilson, to endorse the suffrage amendment, Paul decided that a new tactic was required.

On January 10, 1917, a few well-dressed women planted themselves on both sides of the gates of the White House. They did not speak but stood motionless holding banners that asked, MR. PRESI-DENT, WHAT WILL YOU DO FOR WOMAN SUFFRAGE? and HOW LONG MUST WOMEN WAIT FOR LIBERTY?

If this was not the first time pickets stood outside the White House, it was certainly something new to see women of such obvi-ous social standing doing it. The next day the pickets appeared

Three women picketing in front of the White House, 1917

again, and it was clear that they intended to stay until they got their questions answered. Unsure how to respond, the police allowed them to stay. The president often tipped his hat as his car passed through the gates.

Things began to change in April when the United States declared war on Germany. The Wilson administration launched a propaganda campaign to support the war that whipped the country into a patriotic frenzy.

While some moderate mainstream suffragists set aside their advocacy for the duration of the war, Paul and the members of her organization, the Woman's Party, turned up the heat. The pickets held banners that were increasingly critical of the government. To Wilson's claim that the country was fighting for democracy, one declared, DEMOCRACY BEGINS AT HOME. Another called him KAISER WILSON.

Men in uniform and other passersby began to harass the pickets, tearing the banners from their hands. The police arrived, and instead of defending the women's right to assembly and free expression, they arrested them for obstructing sidewalk traffic. Over the next year, authorities took into custody more than five hundred protestors. Judges sentenced 168 to jail terms ranging from a few days to seven months.

Paul used the arrests to draw national attention to the issue of women's rights. As rapidly as the police arrested pickets, she found fresh ones. She made sure the press received details of the wretched conditions in the prisons where the women were held and the brutal treatment they received from the guards.

Then she joined them. During her trial, Paul and her co-defendants refused to cooperate with the proceedings, remaining silent throughout. Paul spoke only once. "We do not consider ourselves subject to this Court since, as an unenfranchised [sic] class, we have nothing to do with the making of the laws which have put us in this position," she said. [66]

In jail, she demanded to be recognized as a political prisoner and started a hunger strike. Prison officials responded by force-feeding her three times a day. Guards placed her in solitary confinement and threatened her with commitment to an insane asylum.

The suffering paid off. Sympathetic newspaper coverage shifted public opinion. People were no longer blaming the suffragists for their stubbornness. They were angry at the government for punishing women who were fighting for their rights. All of the protesters were released in late November.

Paul, who was in the third week of her hunger strike, appeared frail but triumphant. A few weeks earlier, Wilson had announced that he had changed his mind and would support the federal suffrage amendment, which was named in honor of Susan B. Anthony, who had died in 1906. The House of Representatives approved the Anthony Amendment in January 2018. The Senate agreed and sent it to the states for ratification. On August 26, 1920, the Nineteenth Amendment was ratified. Women had not been given the vote — they had won it.

———

During the Martyr Age, activists had used their right to free speech to curb abuses of government power, attack slavery, and advance women's rights. But there was still little appreciation for the role that free speech plays in a democracy. Most Americans welcomed the suppression of anarchists and other radicals. When the United States went to war in 1917, dissent became a crime.

FIGHTING FOR FREE SPEECH

On the evening of November 2, 1909, James P. Thompson, a member of the Industrial Workers of the World (IWW), climbed onto a soapbox in Spokane, Washington, and began to speak. After months of fighting with city officials over the right to give public addresses in the downtown area, the IWW decided to defy a city ordinance by holding meetings around the clock.

Thompson was only able to say a few words before a policeman pulled him down. Another man immediately took his place and was also arrested. A line of IWW members stood ready to replace every arrested speaker. By the end of the night, 150 people were in jail, including 3 women. Frank Little had attempted to read something. At his hearing, the judge asked what it was. "The Declaration of Independence," Little said. He was sentenced to thirty days in jail.[1]

City officials were not satisfied with arresting those who violated the ban on speaking. They also raided the IWW headquarters, seized four of its leaders, and shut down the offices of a newspaper, the *Industrial Worker*, which had been started when IWW members were first forbidden to speak in the street.

The next day local authorities said their actions had rid the city of a source of "violence and conspiracy." But the fight was only beginning. The IWW sent out a call to "Wobblies" everywhere. "Big free speech fight in Spokane; come yourselves if possible, and bring the boys with you!" it urged.[2]

The night of November 3 more speakers appeared and were arrested. They were replaced by IWW members from around the

Pacific Northwest who had hitched rides on freight trains. "Still they come and still they try to speak," a local newspaper moaned. The jail quickly filled with more than four hundred men.[3]

The free speech fight in Spokane was front-page news in newspapers across the country. Supporters of the American labor movement had not had much to celebrate for many years. Many obstacles confronted unionizing efforts. Most industrial workers were immigrants who didn't speak English, posing communication challenges, and they were usually unskilled, making them easy to replace.

As a result, workers were poorly paid and afraid of losing what little they had. According to a government report, between 25 and 33 percent of working families received too little to support "anything like a comfortable decent condition." A majority of laborers were unemployed for as many as ten weeks per year.[4]

The energy and excitement around the IWW's organizing efforts in 1905 came from its commitment to organize unskilled workers. At the time, the American Federation of Labor, which represented skilled workers and had little interest in helping the rest of the working class, was the only truly national union.

The goal of the IWW was the formation of "One Big Union." It was an openly revolutionary party that sought to replace capitalism with worker control. Unlike the Communist Party that would emerge in 1917, however, the IWW leaders thought change could be accomplished peacefully through a general strike.

Since the strike would only be successful if all workers joined, its organizers focused on recruiting those who were the hardest to enlist, including women in the garment trades and the men who made up the migrant workforce in the mining, lumber, and agricultural industries.

Where some saw hope in the IWW's work, others saw danger. The conflict between capital and labor had already generated some of the most horrific acts of violence in American history.

In 1892, striking steelworkers had opened fire on barges that were being used to bring non-union men to the Carnegie mills in Homestead, Pennsylvania. Two years later, thirty-eight were killed in the Pullman railroad strike.

The courts routinely intervened in labor disputes on the side of capital by issuing injunctions to control strikers. While judges argued that injunctions were necessary to preserve public peace, the list of prohibitions was so broad that it was often impossible for workers to defend their rights. An injunction in a Seattle case barred strikers from

using in any way any language tending to incite the defendant's auditors, or the public, to lawlessness, or tending in any way to arouse the anger and incite the antagonism or wrath of the citizens; and also from using any violence or abusive language of any kind toward the United States Government, the State of Washington, or the city of Seattle, or its public officials, and from using language ridiculing the institutions of this country and holding them up to ridicule.

Judicial injunctions suppressed strikes altogether or limited union activity to the point that the public was unaware that strikes were under way.[5]

In Spokane, the business community was prepared to use every weapon at its disposal to silence the IWW, including brute force. Many Wobblies arrived in jail covered in blood. Some had "teeth kicked out, eyes blackened and clothes torn." One man's jaw was broken.[6]

More than two dozen Wobblies were crammed into a cell that was only eight feet long and six feet wide. It took four policemen to close the door. The prisoners were exposed to so much steam heat that some fainted where they stood. Later the Wobblies were moved to ice-cold cells.

As the number of prisoners grew, the city found additional jail space in an unheated school. Provided with only bread and water, many fell ill. Three hundred ended up in the hospital. Some were so weak they were unable to walk when they were released. Three men died.

But mistreatment only made the Wobblies more resolute. They tormented their captors by singing "La Marseillaise," the anthem of the French Revolution, as well as contemporary songs from *The Little Red Songbook*, a popular IWW publication. At all hours of the day and night, they sang so loudly that people in neighboring buildings complained. Prisoners were expected to break rocks as part of their punishment, but the Wobblies refused. They staged hunger strikes to protest prison conditions.

At the pinnacle of the protest, the taxpayers of Spokane were paying a fortune to feed and house the prisoners. They tried to release them, but the Wobblies refused freedom until they had been granted a jury trial. Even leaving the jail doors open was not enough of an inducement. One man who sneaked away to see his wife begged to be readmitted when he found the jail door had been locked again.

Elizabeth Gurley Flynn, a pregnant nineteen-year-old, became a symbol of the resistance. She was the daughter of Irish immigrants who had given her first speech four years earlier at a Socialist meeting in New York City on the topic "What Socialism Will Do for Women." A few months later, police arrested her and her father for making speeches without a permit on one of the streets in Manhattan's Theater District.

When the prominent theater producer David Belasco learned of the arrest of the attractive young woman, he asked to meet her. He wanted to know if she was interested in being an actress. "Indeed not!" Flynn replied. "I'm in the labor movement and I speak my own piece." By 1909, Elizabeth had become an IWW organizer and the leader of a successful free speech fight in Missoula, Montana.[7]

Flynn and her husband arrived in Spokane two weeks after the battle began. Everyone could see that she was pregnant, and IWW leaders decided that it would be unseemly for her to speak publicly. She was unhappy with the decision, but a new round of arrests soon thrust her into the heart of the fight.

The authorities had decided to suppress the *Industrial Worker* by arresting all eight of its staff members and even some of its newsboys. When Flynn took over the job of putting out the paper, police charged her with conspiracy and took her to jail.

The IWW lost no time in publicizing the imprisonment of its "Joan of Arc." Newspapers across the country couldn't get enough of "the beauteous, black-haired firebrand." More Wobblies began to arrive. "Logging crews of pine camps deserted in a body to Spokane," according to an IWW publication.[8]

At her trial, Flynn made it clear that the First Amendment was at stake. When the judge asked her what she based her speeches on, she replied, "The Bill of Rights." "But you're not a lawyer. How can you interpret them?" the judge asked. "They are in plain English, your honor, anyone can understand them," Flynn replied. "They were not written for lawyers but for the people!"[9]

In February 1910, the Spokane IWW Free Speech Committee announced that it was preparing to launch "new full scale invasions to fill Spokane jails and bull-pens." But city officials, who had already made more than twelve hundred arrests, had had enough and accepted almost all of the IWW's demands. The charges against Wobblies were dropped and all prisoners released. IWW speakers resumed their recruitment efforts on downtown streets.[10]

The free speech fight in Spokane was a significant victory for the IWW. It encouraged its members in cities around the country to challenge ordinances that restricted their right to organize workers. More than a dozen free speech fights took place over the next four years.

The experience of Spokane also established the effectiveness of passive resistance as a protest tactic. Opponents of the IWW had tried to portray members of the organization as violent revolutionists, but the brutality of the Spokane police showed clearly that city officials, not the Wobblies, were guilty of violence. Public support for the IWW grew.

Passive resistance could be dangerous. In some cities, vigilantes responded to IWW invasions. A mob of as many as a thousand men severely beat Wobblies in Fresno and then marched to the outskirts of town and burned down the IWW's tent camp.

In San Diego, the police handed over unionists to vigilantes who beat them and then expelled them from the city. In one of the most notorious incidents, men with guns and clubs stopped a freight train carrying 140 Wobblies at the city limits. They forced the IWW men from the train, made them kiss the American flag, and then ran them through a gauntlet of more than a hundred vigilantes who beat them mercilessly with clubs and sent them back the way they came.

Although the IWW would stage more free speech fights over the next several years, the threat of extralegal violence helped persuade its leadership to concentrate scarce resources on organizing workers.

A Civil Liberties Meltdown

On April 4, 1917, the United States declared war on Germany, thrusting itself into a three-year-old conflict that had already taken the lives of millions. World War I would continue for another eighteen months. While the number of American casualties was relatively small compared to those suffered by Europeans, American life changed dramatically.

President Woodrow Wilson announced that no sacrifice was too great to defeat the autocratic Germans and make the world "safe for democracy." The US government took control of industry to ensure that Allied troops would have everything they needed to defeat "the Huns."

Citizens were expected to play their part. Yet millions of Americans opposed the war. Wobblies and members of the Socialist Party believed workers were dying in a capitalist struggle. Wilson also considered immigrants a grave threat to the war effort. More than five million German immigrants, many of whom had cherished memories of the fatherland, lived in the US, as well as several million Irish immigrants who despised our ally, Great Britain, and hungered for its defeat.

The president issued a warning shortly before the declaration of war. "There are citizens of the United States, I blush to admit, born under other flags . . . who have poured the poison of disloyalty into the very arteries of our national life," Wilson declared. Something would have to be done about any US residents who failed to support the war.[11]

A new law, the Espionage Act, made it a crime to "willfully make false statements with intent to interfere with the operation or success of the military or naval forces." Violations were punishable with a fine of up to $10,000 and twenty years in prison.

At first, the statute occasioned little controversy, perhaps because it seemed to threaten only enemy agents. However, the Espionage Act gave the post office broad new powers to exclude from the mails any material "advocating or urging treason, insurrection, or forcible resistance to any law of the United States."

Leaders of the Free Speech League, which sought changes in the Comstock Act, urged Congress to amend the law's language. "I know what a tremendous instrument of tyranny this rather innocent looking provision of the bill will become," a league attorney wrote Senator Robert La Follette of Wisconsin. No other organization expressed concern.[12]

Postmaster General Albert S. Burleson immediately began using his new power to exclude from the mail any material that was critical of the war. In July, post office officials notified the editors of *The Masses*, a lively literary and political magazine with Socialist leanings, that they could not mail their August issue. When Max Eastman, the editor, demanded to know what articles violated the Espionage Act, officials refused to tell him.

The Masses challenged the post office in court, forcing it to reveal the reasons for rejecting the August issue. The government lawyer pointed to four written items and four cartoons.

The written items included a poem that praised Emma Goldman and Alexander Berkman, two notorious anarchists; an editorial that mentioned their recent arrest; another editorial about the importance of maintaining individualism during a time of war;

and a collection of letters from imprisoned conscientious objectors in Britain.

One cartoon, "Conscription," showed the evils of war. "War Plans" revealed a group of businessmen studying plans in a congressional meeting room while members of Congress, watching from the sidelines, asked, "Where do we come in?"

For the duration of the war, Burleson would decide what newspapers and magazines were delivered to the American people. "For instance, papers may not say that the Government is controlled by Wall Street or munitions manufacturers, or any other special interests," he explained. "We will not permit the publication or circulation of anything hampering the war's prosecution or attacking improperly our allies."[13]

He mainly targeted socialist newspapers, banning at least one issue of twenty-two publications. *The Masses* was forced to close when it was denied use of the mails.

Burleson also tried to suppress *The Milwaukee Leader*, a newspaper published by Victor Berger, a Socialist member of Congress. The post office even refused to deliver mail to the *Leader*, a tactic it occasionally employed against "disloyal" parties although it lacked any legal authority to do so. The foreign-language press generally avoided any commentary on the war from a fear of violating another repressive law, the Trading with the Enemies Act.

The Justice Department was also busy. Its agents obtained search warrants for IWW offices all over the country. At the time, the Wobblies were full of optimism for their future. The European war had created a boom in demand for American products, giving many workers the power to demand higher wages.

The IWW was well positioned to benefit from the boom since it had been successful in organizing workers in several of the fastest-growing industries — agriculture, forestry, and mining. Its membership rose from ten thousand to one hundred thousand. The September 1917 raids that the federal government orchestrated nationwide were shocking. The Wobblies had a long history of conflict with hostile employers and local authorities, but they had never faced opposition from the federal government. Justice Department lawyers showed up with sweeping search warrants that allowed them to seize almost everything in the IWW offices. They occupied the IWW headquarters in Chicago as well as its regional offices, making it virtually impossible for the union to conduct its business. In many cases, federal officers arrested union officials on the spot and denied them bail.

The Wobblies struggled to understand what they had done wrong. On paper, the IWW was a revolutionary organization dedicated to the destruction of capitalism. Some of its leaders had endorsed sabotage in industrial disputes. The IWW condemned the European war. But the organization had not officially opposed American intervention or done anything to obstruct the draft. The Justice Department's investigation turned up no evidence that the union or its members had engaged in any criminal acts.

Nevertheless, the United States government indicted 166 IWW officials in Chicago and 100 more in Wichita, Omaha, Fresno, and Sacramento. The defendants were charged with violating eleven federal laws. Their real crime was "the seditious and disloyal character and teaching of the organization," according to a memo prepared for the attorney general.[14]

In Chicago, more than 113 Wobblies were tried together. Although the proceedings lasted four months, the jury took only an hour to convict them on all charges. The judge sentenced the top officials to twenty years in prison. "When the country is at peace, it is a legal right of free speech to oppose going to war. . . . But once war is declared this right ceases," he declared.[15]

The prosecution of the IWW was only the tip of the iceberg. In just eighteen months, the Justice Department indicted 2,168 people under the Espionage Act and convicted 1,055. The victims included leaders of the Socialist Party like Rose Pastor Stokes, who

Uncle Sam rounding up men labeled "Spy," "Traitor," "IWW," "Germ[an] money," and "Sinn Fein" with the United States Capitol in the background and a flag that reads "Sedition law passed"

was convicted of writing a letter to the editor of a St. Louis newspaper defending the right to dissent from the war. Her alleged crime was writing, "I am for the people and the government is for the profiteers."[16]

Eugene V. Debs, the four-time Socialist Party candidate for president, was sentenced to ten years for a speech he made in Canton, Ohio. Although Debs chose his words carefully, knowing that government stenographers were present at every speech he gave, he was convicted for saying, "[Y]ou need . . . to know that you are fit for something better than slavery and cannon fodder." Debs served two and a half years in prison. In 1920, he ran for president from his prison cell and received more than nine hundred thousand votes.[17]

The overwhelming majority of prosecutions involved ordinary people. The country was in a war fever, and the Justice Department was under tremendous pressure to take action against every manifestation of disloyalty. "German agents are everywhere," warned a magazine ad placed by the Committee on Public Information, a government agency. "Report the man who spreads pessimistic stories . . . cries for peace or belittles our efforts to win the war."[18]

Propaganda was hardly necessary. Every day newspapers published lists of dead and wounded Americans, and Justice Department officials in local field offices across the country were flooded with reports of traitorous words.

Thirty German Americans in South Dakota went to jail for sending a petition to the governor urging reforms in the draft laws. An Iowa man received a twenty-year term for circulating a petition urging the defeat of a congressman who had voted for the draft. Another Iowa man was sent to jail for a year for attending a radical meeting, applauding, and contributing twenty-five cents.

Many Americans believed the government needed their help in policing disloyalty. They joined dozens of private organizations that hunted spies, captured "slackers" who had not registered for the draft, and demanded that everyone purchase their fair share of Liberty bonds.

The American Protective League had 250,000 members who carried badges that said they were members of the "Secret Service." US attorney general Thomas W. Gregory explained that their job was "keeping an eye on disloyal individuals and making reports of disloyal utterances." In practice, they acted as vigilantes, pulling people off the street for questioning and searching homes without warrants.[19]

Whether acting through organized groups, in mobs formed at the spur of the moment, or as outraged individuals, the self-styled patriots often used violence against those they considered to be their enemies. Mobs tarred and feathered people they thought to be disloyal, many of whom were German immigrants.

They beat Charles Klinge and forced him to kiss the flag in Salisbury, Pennsylvania, for remarks he had made about the war and tarred and feathered George Koetzer and tied him to a brass cannon in a park in San Jose, California. A group of drunken miners in Collinsville, Illinois, lynched Robert Prager, a German immigrant and Socialist.

"This Alleged Democracy"

The attacks on free speech did not end with the war on November 11, 1918. One year later, on November 7, 1919, Mitchel Lavrowsky was teaching a class in algebra to a room full of Russian immigrants at the Russian People's House in New York. The fifty-year-old Lavrowsky had been a teacher and principal of the Iglitsky High School in Odessa before immigrating to the United States and now lived quietly with his wife and two children in the Bronx. He had applied for American citizenship.

That didn't matter to the men who entered his classroom with their guns drawn around 8:00 P.M. They identified themselves as agents of the US Department of Justice and ordered everyone to stand.

One of them advanced on Lavrowsky and instructed him to remove his eyeglasses. He struck the teacher in the head. Two more agents joined the assault, beating him until he could not stand and then throwing him down the stairs where more men continued to hit him with pieces of wood they had torn from of the bannister.

Several hundred people, most of them students, were in the Russian People's House that night. The agents of the Justice Department ordered them out of their classrooms and into a gauntlet of men who struck some of them on the head and pushed them down the stairs toward waiting police wagons. Police grabbed students as they approached the school and dragged them inside; others were beaten in the street.

Meanwhile, with the help of New York City police detectives, the Justice Department men began to tear the place apart, breaking furniture, destroying typewriters, and overturning desks and bookshelves until the floor was covered in a sea of paper. When they judged that nothing useful remained, they carted off two hundred prisoners.

The roundup of Russians continued through the night and into the next day in cities across the country. Police burst into apartments and dragged people from their beds. Sometimes they had warrants, but usually they simply arrested everyone they found. In the end, more than a thousand people had been grabbed at the behest of the Justice Department.

The nation was enduring a wrenching conversion to peace, and the public largely cheered the November raids. Unemployment had surged as returning veterans sought to reclaim their old jobs. Consumer goods were growing scarce, no new housing had been built in more than eighteen months, and when Americans could least afford it, they found themselves facing high inflation.

At a time when Americans were feeling vulnerable, the success of the 1917 Bolshevik revolution appeared to have launched a worldwide radical threat that many people easily connected with the growing number of strikes in the United States — more than thirty-six hundred in 1919 alone. Although these strikes were driven by inflation and other economic realities, not radical ideology, employers did their best to paint workers who advocated for better pay and conditions as subversives.

The threat of revolution seemed to be confirmed when eight bombs exploded outside the homes of prominent men, including A. Mitchell Palmer, the new attorney general, in June 1919. The nation demanded swift action, and the so-called Palmer Raids were the result that November. A second, even larger series of raids that seized more than three thousand members of two new American parties, the Communist Party and the Communist Labor Party, followed in January 1920.

Although the Palmer Raids generated a lot of good publicity for the Department of Justice, they accomplished little. The government never discovered who was behind the June bombings. In the absence of any evidence of criminal activity by the radicals arrested in the raids, foreign nationals who had been taken into custody were ordered to be deported. But the US Department of Labor later canceled thousands of deportation orders, and in the end, the government succeeded in exiling only eight hundred of the more than four thousand people it had arrested.

The government raids did achieve something important, however. They caused a growing number of Americans to recognize that the freedoms promised by the First Amendment could not be taken for granted. They had to be fought for. Emma Goldman was one of the people who understood this best.

Born in Russia, the fifty-year-old Goldman was one of the country's most notorious radicals. Like many anarchists, she believed that violent acts were a legitimate response to capitalist oppression. Her lover, Alexander Berkman, was sent to prison for attempting to assassinate the manager of the Carnegie Steel Mill during a bitter strike. Goldman herself once horsewhipped a political opponent, but mostly she used her great oratorical gifts to apply the lash.

Conservatives had longed for years to send "Red Emma" packing, and the Red Scare gave them their chance. Released from a prison term for opposing the war, Goldman was swiftly arrested again and held for deportation. John Edgar Hoover, a twenty-four-year-old Department of Justice official who was helping plan Palmer's anti-radical campaign, had urged the move.

If Hoover hoped to hear Goldman plead for mercy during her deportation hearing, he was disappointed. She refused to speak.

Emma Goldman (standing in car) speaks about birth control at Union Square Park, 1916

Instead, in a statement that was read on her behalf by her attorney, Goldman attacked the effort to deport foreign radicals as a threat to free speech.

"Ever since I have been in this country — and I have lived here practically all my life — it has been dinned into my ears that under the institutions of this alleged Democracy one is entirely free to think and feel as he pleases," Goldman's lawyer read. "What becomes of this sacred guarantee of freedom of thought and conscience when persons are being persecuted and driven out for the very motives and purposes for which the pioneers who built up this country laid down their lives?"[20]

Goldman warned that the government was making a terrible mistake by confusing conformity with security. "The free expression of the hopes and aspirations of a people is the greatest and only safety in a sane society," she said. "In truth, it is such free expression and discussion alone that can point the most beneficial path for human progress and development." Two months later, Hoover, the future leader of the Federal Bureau of Investigation, watched as Goldman, Berkman, and 247 other radicals departed under armed guard on a boat bound for Russia.[21]

Radicals were not the only ones talking about the importance of free speech. Deeply distressed by the failure of the judicial system to protect civil liberties during the war, defense lawyers and law school professors began to speak up too.

Although it seems surprising today, the courts had not handled many cases involving the First Amendment. There were few legal decisions protecting free expression rights that could serve as precedents in the cases that were now coming before the courts.

Judges fell back on a tradition of punishing speech that had a "bad tendency." "It is true that disapproval of the war and the advocacy for peace are not crimes under the Espionage Act," a federal appeals court acknowledged, "... but the question here is whether the nature and probable tendency and effect of the words ... are such as are calculated to produce the result condemned by the statute."[22]

The courts left it to juries to decide whether the speech in question was harmful. During the war, jurors usually convicted.

A Free Trade in Ideas

In the summer of 1918, a thirty-two-year-old professor at Harvard Law School began a systematic study of the use of the Espionage Act to suppress political speech. Zechariah D. Chafee Jr. was a very unlikely candidate to emerge as the champion of the First Amendment rights of Socialists, Wobblies, and other radicals. Chafee's father was a wealthy iron manufacturer. "My family is a family that has money," Chafee would say later. "I believe in property and I believe in making money."[23]

Chafee's article, "Freedom of Speech," appeared in the *New Republic* on November 16, 1918, five days after the war ended. It was the opening shot in a campaign to create a legal and political defense of free speech.

Chafee agreed with Emma Goldman that the country had made a mistake. "[J]udges . . . have interpreted the 1917 Act so broadly as to make practically all opposition to the war criminal," he wrote. As a result, courts had suppressed a freedom at the core of democracy. "One of the most important purposes of society and government is the discovery and spread of truth on subjects of general concern. This is possible only through absolutely unlimited discussion."[24]

Chafee acknowledged that government had other purposes that potentially clashed with free speech — maintaining order, educating the young, providing for national defense. Yet he insisted that protecting freedom of speech was just as important: "Unlimited discussion sometimes interferes with these purposes, which must then be balanced against freedom of speech, but freedom of speech ought to weigh heavily in the balance. The First Amendment gives binding force to this principle of political wisdom."

During the war, judges had not attempted to strike a balance: They had punished any speech that could undermine the war effort. But speech must be free even in wartime, Chafee insisted. "The pacifists and socialists are wrong now, but they may be right the next time," he said. "The only way to find out whether a war is unjust is to let people say so."[25]

Chafee was surely heartbroken several months later when the US Supreme Court considered the constitutionality of the Espionage Act for the first time. In three cases, it endorsed the use of the bad tendency test during wartime and upheld long jail sentences for opponents of the war who had urged people to exercise their democratic rights.

Justice Oliver Wendell Holmes Jr. wrote the opinions in all three cases for a unanimous court. A veteran of the Civil War, the seventy-seven-year-old Holmes, who sported a luxuriant white handlebar mustache, was the oldest justice and possessed one of the best legal minds on the court. In 1905, he had rejected the deep conservatism of his colleagues by voting to uphold a pioneering

New York statute that limited the labor of bakery workers to ten hours per day.

It was because Holmes was so respected that his opinions in the Espionage Act cases were deeply disappointing to civil libertarians. In *Schenck v. US*, Holmes observed that the First Amendment's protection of the right of free speech was obviously not absolute. "The most stringent protection of free speech would not protect a man in falsely shouting fire in a crowded theater, and causing a panic," he wrote. The government had a right to limit words that posed "a clear and present danger" of disrupting the war effort.[26]

However, soon after delivering this decision and another that sent Eugene Debs to jail, Holmes began having second thoughts. He drafted, but never sent, a letter to the editor of the *New Republic* responding to criticism of his decisions. "I hated to have to write the Debs case and still more those of the other poor devils before us the same day and the week before," he wrote. " . . . I think it is quite possible that if I had been on the jury I should have been for acquittal."[27]

Amid the Red Scare panic, Holmes corresponded with friends who urged him to rethink his position. After reading a new article by Chafee, he met with the young man for tea at his home.

On November 10, the US Supreme Court handed down another decision affirming the power of the government to punish speech under the Espionage Act. In the case of *Abrams v. US*, it upheld long prison terms for four immigrants who had printed and distributed a pamphlet calling on workers to strike in protest over the use of American troops in Siberia, which they interpreted as an attempt to undermine the Russian Revolution.

This time the decision was not unanimous. Holmes wrote a dissenting opinion joined by Louis Brandeis that questioned the danger posed by "the surreptitious publishing of a silly pamphlet by an unknown man."[28]

The other justices were so disturbed by the prospect of a dissent by Holmes that three of them visited him at his home and tried to dissuade him. Holmes's wife, Fanny, joined the discussion and urged her husband to change his mind. But Holmes politely declined.

In the *Schenck* case, Holmes had first enunciated the idea that speech could be restricted when it posed "a clear and present danger" to the country. In his dissent, he made it clear that such a threat would only exist under very narrow circumstances.

"It is only the present danger of immediate evil or an intent to bring it about that warrants Congress in setting a limit to the expression of opinion," he said. That danger did not exist in the *Abrams* case, Holmes said. Although he did not say so, the implication was clear that he no longer believed that threat had existed in the vast majority of the Espionage Act cases.[29]

The dissent by Holmes and Brandeis didn't help the defendants in the *Abrams* case. They were sent to prison and eventually deported. But it meant a great deal to those who were fighting to expand protections for free speech.

In the final paragraph of his opinion, Holmes embraced the view advanced by Chafee and others that unfettered debate is the only way to attain truth. He called for "a free trade in ideas." "[T]he best test of truth is the power of the thought to get itself accepted in the competition of the market," he said.

He acknowledged that there was a risk involved, but it was a risk that is inherent in democratic government: "It is an experiment, as all life is an experiment. Every year if not every day we have to wager our salvation upon some prophecy based upon imperfect knowledge. While that experiment is part of our system I think we should be eternally vigilant against attempts to check the expression of opinions that we loathe and believe to be fraught with death."[30]

Free speech advocates were overjoyed. Holmes had given the cause of free speech two things it badly needed: prestige and an eloquence that would inspire others to take up the fight.

The American Civil Liberties Union was founded two months after Holmes issued his historic dissent. Its organizers were men and women who came together during the war to help the thousands of pacifists who had been drafted into the army. They were sent to military camps where they were frequently beaten and jailed in an effort to force them to fight. It also tried to assist the victims of mob violence and protested the growing government suppression of speech.

The leader of the ACLU was Roger Nash Baldwin, a thirty-six-year-old man who had grown up with every advantage. Born in Wellesley Hills, a suburb of Boston, his family was wealthy enough to free him from any concern about making a living.

It was also a family that encouraged liberal ideas. "I was aware of Emerson, Thoreau and the Alcotts about as soon as I was aware of any intellectual figures," Baldwin said. "They were household names." He hoped to emulate men who had defied convention. "I sought character, personality, uniqueness," he said.[31]

After graduating from Harvard College, Baldwin entered the new field of social work. One of his professors recommended him for a job in St. Louis, where he became the head of a settlement house and was given the responsibility of establishing a department of sociology at Washington University despite never having taken a course in the subject.

He had an abundance of self-confidence, and his willingness to accept new challenges served him well. Just a year after his arrival in St. Louis, the judge who headed the city's new juvenile court offered him the chance to become the court's first chief probation officer. To meet the challenge of overseeing the rehabilitation of two thousand children, Baldwin assembled a staff of fifteen probation officers, most of whom were older than him.

Baldwin quickly became frustrated. Social workers and probation officers attempted to help people without recommending any way to eliminate the poverty that was the source of their problems. He was also skeptical of radicals until friends dragged him to hear a speech by Emma Goldman. It was a revelation. "Here was a vision of the end of poverty and injustice by free association of those who worked, by the abolition of privilege, and by the organized power of the exploited," Baldwin recalled many years later.[32]

"I was for the underdog, whoever he was, by training and instinct, and I had an endless capacity for indignation at injustice," he said. "Any challenge to freedom aroused me and I was not satisfied until I acted."[33]

This passion led him to provide bail for Wobblies who had been jailed for refusing to pay for their meals in local restaurants. (They told the owners to bill the mayor.) It also prompted him to take up his first free speech case. When Margaret Sanger was barred from speaking at a private hall, Baldwin convinced her to present her address on the steps of the building.

Baldwin believed that people like Goldman and Sanger moved mankind forward. "I am dead certain that human progress depends on those heretics, rebels, and dreamers . . . whose 'holy discontent' has challenged established authority and created the expanding visions mankind may yet realize," he said.[34]

Baldwin had embarked on his civil liberties career in April 1917. A pacifist, he volunteered his services to American Union Against Militarism (AUAM), which was fighting a losing battle to keep the United States out of the war. "How and where in your judgment could you use me?" he asked in a letter. He also said he would work for free. A short while later, he arrived in New York and took charge of the National Civil Liberties Bureau (NCLB), a part of the AUAM.[35]

As the fight for the rights of conscientious objectors grew into a struggle for the civil liberties of everyone who was critical of the war, Baldwin battled against the appearance of disloyalty. "We want also to look like patriots in everything we do," he explained to a colleague. "We want to get a lot of flags, talk a good deal about the Constitution and what our forefathers wanted to make of this country."[36]

But conflict with the government was inevitable. When the leaders of the IWW were brought to trial, the NCLB published *The Truth About the IWW*. The pamphlet rejected the charges of sedition against the Wobblies.

Federal officials were outraged that the NCLB would defend an organization that they viewed as obviously bent on the country's destruction. Some considered Baldwin and his colleagues outright traitors. The post office blocked the mailing of NCLB pamphlets. The Justice Department raided the NCLB offices. When an attorney tried to block the search, an agent drew his gun and ordered him to stand aside.

The Justice Department seriously considered indicting Baldwin and members of the NCLB board of directors. But the war was almost over. Cooler heads opposed legal action against an organization that defended civil liberties. In the end, only Baldwin went to jail. He had refused to be drafted, which he readily admitted in a statement he read at his trial. He was sentenced to a year in jail.

When Baldwin emerged from prison in July 1919, he was more determined than ever to pursue the fight for the working class. Only a few weeks after getting married, he spent several months getting a taste of life as a laborer. In Chicago, Baldwin joined the Cooks and Waiters Union and marched on picket lines outside steel mills. Then he jumped on a freight train headed for St. Louis; shoveled ore into the smelter at a lead mine in Missouri; worked for a railroad for a couple of days in Youngstown, Ohio; and ended up cleaning ovens in a steel mill in Homestead, Pennsylvania.

When he returned to New York to resume the fight for civil liberties, he was convinced that the biggest battle would be the one for workers' rights. "The cause we now serve is labor," Baldwin wrote in a memo to the board of the new ACLU.[37]

The chief weapon would be publicity. The ACLU would join the battle where it was being fought — in the field. It would send "a few well known liberals" to challenge restrictions on union meetings in the Pennsylvania coal fields, where their arrests "would dramatize the situation effectively." The board approved the plan on January 12, 1920.[38]

For an organization that was hoping to win public support, the timing could hardly have been worse. The Justice Department had just arrested thousands of radicals in its second and largest series of raids. Nevertheless, the ACLU opened for business a week later, operating on the ground floor of a three-story brick house on West 13th Street in New York.

The ACLU's first major battle would prove to be one of its severest tests. Baldwin had been reading about the struggle that the United Mine Workers was waging to organize the miners of Mingo County, West Virginia. In March, he hired journalist John L. Spivak to go to West Virginia, meet with union officials, and make recommendations to the executive committee on ways that the ACLU might support organizing efforts there.

Spivak was horrified by what he saw and urged the ACLU to produce leaflets, posters, and bulletins denouncing the coal operators in the strongest possible language. Spivak sent along a draft bulletin that demanded "[t]he thugs and gunmen of Logan County must go!"

When the executive committee hesitated to use such strong language, Spivak pleaded with Baldwin to get it to see things as they really were. "They are still under the impression that there is some semblance of legal procedure here," he wrote. "There is not. You can't hold a meeting here, get pinched and then fight it out in the courts. If you try to hold a meeting in the southern counties, you'll never live to see the courts. . . ."[39]

Spivak wasn't exaggerating. Not long afterward a shootout between union supporters and company detectives killed ten men in the town of Matewan.

The Matewan massacre was the ACLU's first opportunity to project itself into a national controversy, and Baldwin seized it. When the sheriff who had sided with the miners was indicted for murder, Baldwin told his attorney that the ACLU would handle publicity during the trial, doing everything possible to build public support for the miners. Meanwhile, it pressed for a congressional investigation of the West Virginia situation.

The ACLU stepped up its efforts in the spring of 1921 when new violence led the governor to declare martial law. The state militia stopped the gunfire, but it also prohibited union meetings, suppressed the union newspaper, and arrested twelve union leaders on a charge of unlawful assembly.

The limits of the ACLU's strategy became apparent again the first time that it sent one of its lawyers into Pennsylvania to protest the ban on union meetings in coal mining towns. In the spring of 1922, Baldwin telephoned New York attorney Arthur Garfield Hays to tell him that the Pennsylvania miners had gone out on strike and asked him to participate in a protest in Vintondale with officials of the United Mine Workers.

Hays, several UMW officials, and two reporters set off in two cars. On reaching Vintondale, the union drivers gunned their engines, rushing by a swearing sentry. They soon heard the clatter of hooves as they were pursued into the center of town by armed horsemen, members of the Coal and Iron Police, a state police force that was paid by the coal operators.

"We know you, you ---- ---- ----," one policeman yelled. "You're union organizers . . . Get the hell out of this town." Hays emerged from his car full of fire. "Who are you men?" he asked. "Where is the post office? Where is the mayor's office? We'd like to see the ordinances of this town."[40]

One pointed to a sign that said the sheriff would arrest anyone who created public disorder. "I see it — what of it?" Hays asked. "I'm going to stand here as long as I damn please."

Hays wasn't standing for long. "Bust this up or we'll bust you up," a policeman shouted. Then, amid hoots, threats, and curses, the police fell on the outsiders. Three men grabbed Hays by the nape of the neck and the seat of his pants and thrust him back in the car. He and the rest of his party beat a hasty retreat.

The ACLU was more successful in its next efforts to support unionism. In 1923, Upton Sinclair, a member of the ACLU national committee, led a campaign to defend striking longshoremen in Los Angeles, one of the most anti-union cities in the country. Famous for writing *The Jungle*, a novel that was a devastating exposé of the meatpacking industry, Sinclair used his celebrity to organize demonstrations that forced police to end their efforts to suppress the strike.

The next year Baldwin helped silk workers in Paterson, New Jersey, to organize protests, including one in which two young sisters carrying the American flag led a march to city hall where someone read the Constitution. Fifty policemen charged the crowd, beating participants with nightsticks. Public outrage forced city officials to lift restrictions on union meetings.

At the end of the 1920s, Roger Baldwin estimated that nine out of ten of the fights that the ACLU had taken on during its first decade involved the rights of labor. But ACLU had never limited itself to fighting for workers. It was committed to uncompromising advocacy of free speech. "There should be no prosecutions for the mere expression of opinion on matters of public concern, however radical, however violent," it stated in its first annual report.[41]

This meant that the ACLU could not just defend its friends. It had to protect the rights of people violently opposed to the liberalism of its members, even those who used their right of free speech to advocate violating the civil liberties of others. In the 1920s, that meant defending the rights of the Ku Klux Klan.

In September 1921, the New York *World* published a three-week exposé of a new threat to the public peace. The newspaper reported that five hundred thousand Americans were members of the recently reborn KKK.

The original Klan organized in the South to restore white supremacy following the Civil War. The new Klan was also deeply racist, but its strongest appeal was to people who feared the influence of "foreigners," the nearly eighteen million immigrants who had arrived in the United States between 1890 and 1914, especially Catholics and Jews.

The *World* exaggerated the Klan's strength, but it did not overstate its appeal. In the following months, partly as a result of the publicity it received from the *World*, the KKK grew with phenomenal speed, reaching one million members a year later. Originally confined to the South, the new Klan had as many members in Ohio, Indiana, and Illinois as there were in the South and Southwest combined. Nor was the Klan confined to rural areas and small towns. It was strongly represented in Indianapolis, Dayton, Portland, Youngstown, Denver, and Dallas.

Efforts to suppress the Ku Klux Klan in 1922 and 1923 presented the first test of the ACLU's commitment to free speech for all. Certainly, there could be no question that the ACLU and the Klan despised each other. Shortly before the publication of the New York *World* exposé of the Klan, Albert DeSilver, the co-director of the ACLU, drew attention to the violence of the Klan in an article in *The Nation*.

DeSilver believed that violence was inherent in the organization. "It is a child conceived in the tradition of a lawless past and brought forth in the extravagant obscurantism of present-day prejudice," he wrote. "Its life cannot and should not be a happy one. The modern Ku Klux Klan does not deserve to live and it had much better die."[42]

It was not easy to stand up for the rights of a group whose organizing principle was prejudice. Even many liberals applauded the

New York legislature when it passed a bill that forced the Klan to reveal the names of its leaders and members, subjecting them to public pressure.

But ACLU leaders believed the principle of free speech must be upheld for all groups if it was to be effective.

In 1920, DeSilver told the leader of the National Association for the Advancement of Colored People (NAACP) that it was "a great mistake" to ask the post office to ban KKK literature from the mails. "We do not think that it is ever a good policy for an organization interested in human liberty to invoke repressive measures against any of its antagonists," DeSilver said. "By doing so it creates a danger of making a precedent against itself."[43]

The ACLU opposed the NAACP's campaign to ban D. W. Griffith's racist classic, *Birth of a Nation*, a film that glorified the deeds of the original Klan. It also criticized the New York Klan registration law and challenged a ban on Klan meetings imposed by Boston mayor James Curley.

In arguing against the meeting ban, the ACLU again warned that repression was a two-edged sword. If Curley could ban the Klan in Boston, "there would be considerable parts of this country in which religious intolerance would prohibit Catholics, Jews, and indeed, the representatives of some Protestant sects, from holding meetings or speaking at all," the Massachusetts Civil Liberties Union told the mayor.[44]

The Klan was not the only group to emerge in the 1920s that attempted to suppress civil liberties. The war and the Red Scare had demonstrated that there was money to be made by fanning the fears of the American people over the threat of Communist subversion. More than a dozen "patriotic" groups competed to lead the fight against radicalism.

The self-styled patriots spent a lot of time worrying about whether teachers were indoctrinating students with foreign ideas.

"A great many of our members write that radicalism has obtained a toe-hold among teachers in public schools," the Better America Federation reported.[45]

Conservatives wanted teachers to promote love of country in the classroom and warned them to refrain from endorsing unorthodox opinions in their private lives as well. Eighteen states demanded some sort of loyalty statement by teachers.

Patriot watchdogs also purged schools of "radical" literature, including magazines like *The Nation* and *New Republic*. The American Legion published its own two-volume history textbook to "inspire the children with patriotism, preach on every page a vivid love of America and preserve the old patriotic legends."[46]

The American Association of University Professors, which had been founded in 1915, emerged as the main defender of academic freedom in colleges. The American Historical Association and the American Sociological Society spoke out against historical distortions.

In 1925, the ACLU learned about the introduction of a bill in the Tennessee legislature that made it a crime to teach evolution in public schools. When the bill passed and was signed into law, the ACLU immediately sent a press release to Tennessee newspapers offering to defend any teacher who defied the law. A short time later, a science teacher named John Scopes stepped forward to accept the offer.

Both the ACLU and the prosecutors hoped to keep the trial focused narrowly on the issue of whether the majority can dictate what is taught in the public schools. Everyone expected the jury to convict Scopes and was looking forward to the argument over academic freedom in the appeals court.

In the meantime, Roger Baldwin intended to take full advantage of publicity about the case. The ACLU brought Scopes east for a couple of appearances in New York and Washington. Tall and slender, the twenty-four-year-old Scopes was both boyish and academic in his horn-rimmed glasses. Photographers posed him in front of the Statue of Liberty and a copy of the Constitution.

Scopes was an instant sensation, according to the New York *World*. "Under the banner of liberalism, to the blaze of page headlines, with the aid of special interviews, posed photographs and human interest incidents, the conglomerate host of liberals is falling in about the lanky, grave-eyed Tennessee high-school teacher," it reported.[47]

The *Scopes* case made it possible for the ACLU to secure the support of some of the most prominent people in American life. It established an advisory committee to assist it in raising funds for the case, inviting twenty leading educators to join. All twenty accepted.

More than two hundred reporters showed up in Tennessee for the opening of the trial; their stories would appear in more than twenty-three hundred dailies.

Ultimately, the *Scopes* case did not succeed in establishing the principle of academic freedom. As expected, the jury convicted Scopes. However, the prosecution was able to persuade the judge to exclude weeks of testimony by the ACLU's scientific experts. The ACLU also lost the chance to appeal Scopes's conviction when the Tennessee Supreme Court dismissed the case because of a technical error.

The anti-evolution crusade continued. The Mississippi legislature banned the teaching of evolution the next year.

Although the ACLU did not win everything it hoped, the *Scopes* case was an important battle for public opinion. It allowed civil libertarians to identify their fight with the struggle for liberty that had begun centuries before when Galileo challenged the authority of the church, and to invoke the memory of the founding fathers, men who had put everything at risk to win the right to think freely.

The *Scopes* case gave Americans a new appreciation of the vulnerability of free speech in a democracy. "The most ominous sign of our time . . . is . . . the growth of an intolerant spirit," Charles Evans Hughes, a former presidential candidate, governor of New York, and US Supreme Court justice, warned several months after Scopes was convicted. "[F]reedom of learning is the vital breath of democracy and progress."[48]

The ACLU was not alone in the fight for free speech. Authors, publishers, librarians, and booksellers were also enlisting.

This was an important change. The publishing community had long believed that its mission was to produce books and magazines that ennobled existence by focusing on eternal values. According to one of the leading American critics of the day, great literature "is that which recognizes the moral conflict as the supreme interest of life, and the message of Christianity as the only real promise of victory."[49]

Few authors before World War I were brave enough to challenge the conventions of genteel society, and the few who did found themselves in trouble with the law.

In 1907, an English romance, *Three Weeks*, became a bestseller in the United States using the kind of language that is found today in TV soap operas. Despite sales that quickly reached fifty thousand copies, a Boston anti-vice group, the Watch and Ward Society, went to court to have the book declared obscene. The judge rejected the publisher's claim that the words *obscene* and *indecent* were vague.

Notwithstanding this victory for good taste, the trickle of "bad" books became a torrent in the 1920s. A new generation of authors like Sherwood Anderson, H. L. Mencken, F. Scott Fitzgerald, Sinclair Lewis, John Dos Passos, and Ben Hecht insisted on showing how life was really lived. This included a willingness to deal more frankly with sex. D. H. Lawrence proclaimed that sex had been unjustly ignored in literature. "Let us hesitate no longer to announce that the sensual passions and mysteries are equally sacred with the spiritual mysteries and passions," he wrote in 1920.[50]

At that moment, James Joyce was in Paris finishing *Ulysses*, a novel that law enforcement authorities would find particularly troubling because it combined the greatest artistic achievement with unprecedented sexual explicitness.

In July 1920, John S. Sumner, Comstock's successor as secretary of the New York Society for the Suppression of Vice, arrested Margaret Anderson and Jane Heap, the editors of the *Little Review*, a literary magazine that had been publishing excerpts from *Ulysses*. The judge fined Anderson and Heap $50 but not before Anderson tried to put the prosecutors on trial. "It was the poet, the artist, who discovered love, created the lover, made sex everything that it is beyond a function," she said. "It is the Mr. Sumners who have made obscenity."[51]

The law had no way to distinguish between pornographic works, whose main purpose was sexual stimulation, and works that included sexual subjects for other purposes. However, things were beginning to change.

The New York courts started to narrow the definition of obscenity, declaring that only books that appealed to a "prurient" or excessive interest in sex could be banned. They also ruled that a book could not be condemned based on isolated passages but must be considered as a whole and allowed defendants to introduce testimony from experts to establish an author's reputation and a book's artistic merit.

Sumner and his supporters responded by attempting to strengthen the New York obscenity law. They formed a Clean Books League to pass a bill to restore the old definition of obscenity. Judge John Ford, one of the organizers, wanted to exclude any opportunity for testimony about the literary value of a challenged work. In his view, the majority had the right to suppress books it regarded as indecent. The question of whether a book is indecent is one to be decided by the "ordinary, common sense, straight-out mind" of the average man, not by a "coterie of literati," he said.[52]

The "clean books" bill made rapid progress in the New York legislature, which had recently approved a film censorship law. No one appeared at the assembly hearing to testify against the book censorship bill, and it was approved by an overwhelming margin.

Critics began to organize only when the bill stood on the verge of passage in the Senate. Alerted to the threat to free expression by an Albany reporter, publisher Horace Liveright spread the alarm. Liveright had a lot at stake. His firm, Boni & Liveright, was one of the new houses most invested in publishing the avant-garde books that most publishers continued to reject. His authors included Eugene O'Neill, Ernest Hemingway, and Theodore Dreiser.

During a hearing before the Senate Judiciary Committee, the critics explained that since any indecent passage condemned a work, the law could suppress the Bible, several dictionaries, and works by Shakespeare, Boccaccio, and Dante.

Infuriated, Ford pointed his finger at the critics. "These publishers, editors and authors profess to be greatly concerned about protecting the Bible and Shakespeare. They don't care about the Bible. All they are interested in is the dirty profits from their own filthy books."[53]

Critics of the clean books bill were encouraged when the judiciary committee agreed to delay a vote on it.

Although opponents had bought some time, they still faced a serious problem. Their base of support was narrow. The largest group in the coalition was the National Publishers Association, representing the magazine industry, which had good reason to believe it would be the first target of stronger obscenity laws. With the launch of *True Story* in 1919, magazine publishers had learned of the tremendous appetite for confessional literature and sexual titillation.

Many in the book industry were not willing to oppose the clean books bill. The National Association of Book Publishers, the major publishing trade association, had refused to follow Liveright into the fray. It did not testify at the hearing and was conspicuously absent from the anti-censorship coalition that organized later.

Book publishers, authors, librarians, and booksellers took pride in their role as purveyors of culture, and many considered it part of their job to protect the public from bad books. As early as 1908, the president of the American Library Association, Arthur Bostwick, warned librarians that immigrants were undermining American literature with "standards of propriety [that] are sometimes those of an earlier and grosser age." The publisher Henry Holt wrote *The New York Times* in 1922 to condemn growing sexual explicitness in literature.[54]

Librarians and booksellers sometimes acted as censors themselves. Following Bostwick's call to arms in 1908, *Library Journal* asked librarians how they were handling requests for bad books and was flooded with suggestions from around the country for ways to thwart dirty-minded readers.

One Atlanta librarian said that she had shelved such books in places where she thought few would find them. If a bad book attained an "unprecedented popularity," it was removed from the shelves and finally discarded.[55]

In 1915, Boston booksellers joined with the Watch and Ward Society to review questionable books. When a committee of three booksellers and three Watch and Ward members agreed that a book was unsuitable, they notified all Massachusetts booksellers, who had forty-eight hours to remove it or face possible prosecution. Newspapers cooperated by refusing to review or advertise banned titles. As a result, at least in the local market, it was almost as if the book had never been published. By 1926, the Boston Booksellers Committee had suppressed between fifty and seventy-five books.

However, attitudes were changing. The controversy over New

York's clean books bill led many in the book industry to rethink their roles.

Booksellers and librarians began to speak up in 1923. At the American Booksellers Association convention, an iconoclastic young bookseller from Detroit, Arthur Proctor, told his colleagues that young people wanted books that portrayed life honestly. "[They] are demanding those books. . . . The responsibility of the bookseller towards his customers is not just to sell books . . . but to get them the books in spite of the censorship . . ." he said.[56]

Mary Rothrock, a young librarian from Knoxville, Tennessee, delivered a similar message at the American Library Association's annual conference. It is not the job of a librarian to measure a book's "possible moral effect on mature readers," she said. It is to bring "to all people the books that belong to them."

Both young book industry professionals touched off storms of protest. Outraged booksellers had Proctor's remarks stricken from the record. Fortunately, the fate of the clean books bill did not depend on a unified industry response. When it was reintroduced, Democrats, who had taken control of the legislature, opposed it.[57]

Their leader in the Senate, James J. Walker, dismissed it with a few words. "No woman was ever ruined by a book," he said. The bill was defeated.[58]

The fight against the clean books bill was a turning point in the attitude of the book industry toward censorship. Both the National Association of Book Publishers and the American Library Association opposed the New York bill when it was reintroduced. At their 1924 convention, booksellers condemned all censorship except "the censorship of intelligent public opinion."[59]

However, another major book censorship battle lay ahead. In 1927, Boston's police chief, Michael Crowley, issued a list of eight novels that he considered obscene despite the fact that they had all been issued by major publishers and were advertised and sold freely elsewhere. "I have read these books, and I think they are bad," he explained.[60]

Crowley also hinted strongly that Dreiser's *American Tragedy* was obscene. When Liveright, Dreiser's publisher, sought a court review, a judge agreed with Chief Crowley. The police also arrested a young bookstore clerk for selling Upton Sinclair's *Oil*, a book about the Teapot Dome scandal, because it contained a reference to birth control.

Booksellers began pulling books from their shelves that they feared might subject them to prosecution. They sent the district attorney fifty-seven bestselling titles and requested an advisory opinion on whether they were obscene. A reporter for *The New York Times* wrote that Boston was facing "a sort of moral panic."[61] By the spring of 1929, Boston had become notorious for its rejection of works that circulated freely in the rest of the country. At least sixty-five books had been suppressed, including works by the philosopher Bertrand Russell and novels by H. G. Wells, Sherwood Anderson, William Faulkner, John Dos Passos, and Ben Hecht.

When *Scribner's Magazine* began serializing Hemingway's *A Farewell to Arms* in the summer of 1929, Crowley banned it. A few months later, the mayor refused to permit a theater to produce Eugene O'Neill's *Strange Interlude*.

"Banned in Boston" had become a national catchphrase, symbolizing narrowness and intolerance.

Representatives of two Boston institutions — *Atlantic Monthly* magazine and publisher Little, Brown — issued a statement denouncing police censorship as "high-handed, erratic and ill-advised."[62]

"Do not make us ridiculous," the *Boston Herald* warned. "Do not imply to the world that those whom we elect to office have no comprehension . . . of intellectual freedom."[63]

Seven hundred supporters of civil liberties attended a banquet at which the actions of the police were ridiculed. As Margaret

Sanger sat at the head table wearing a gag, young men and women paraded around the hall dressed in the costumes of characters from the books that had been banned.

The ACLU at first avoided the fight over book censorship, both in New York and Massachusetts. At the time, its small budget was stretched thin by its efforts to defend the free speech rights of workers.

Also, Roger Baldwin and other Protestant ACLU leaders were puritanical about depictions of sexual activity, and they knew that many ACLU members shared their distaste. "I am wholly in favor of the censorship of books, magazines, plays and movies," a strong ACLU supporter in Boston wrote Baldwin.[64]

The ACLU overcame its reticence about defending sexual material in 1929. The obscenity fight that became the turning point for ACLU, however, involved not a novel but a sex education book.

A member of the Daughters of the American Revolution had ordered a copy of Mary Ware Dennett's pamphlet, *The Sex Side of Life — An Explanation for Young People*, and then complained about its contents to the post office, which charged Dennett with violating the Comstock Act. It took a jury in New York only forty minutes to convict her.

The prosecution of Dennett was widely criticized. *The Sex Side of Life*, which she had written for her sons ten years earlier, contained basic information about sexual organs and intercourse. It also discussed masturbation, which it discouraged.

The book had been distributed privately without causing any protest, and many worried that if it were suppressed, all sexual information was at risk. The *New Republic*, which expressed little concern about the prosecution of *American Tragedy*, was outraged. "The conviction of Mrs. Dennett . . . constitutes a frightful injury not only to a principle, but to the children of this nation and to society itself," it wrote.[65]

The ACLU intervened vigorously in the *Dennett* case. Morris

Ernst, an ACLU attorney, represented the author, and the ACLU organized a Dennett Defense Committee to pay for her other expenses. An appeals court overturned Dennett's conviction in 1930.

By then, the ACLU was deeply involved in the Boston fight. It reorganized its weak Massachusetts affiliate and issued a pamphlet, *The Censorship in Boston,* which called for amending the state obscenity law to allow juries to consider a book as a whole. During a meeting in Boston's Old South Church, Baldwin promised that the ACLU would fight "until all this censorship is abolished in Boston."[66]

The battle over book censorship undermined the enormous prestige the New York Society for the Suppression of Vice, the Watch and Ward Society, and other anti-vice societies had once enjoyed because it demonstrated their inability to distinguish between hard-core pornography and high art.

Some people began to question whether the censors were not acting out their own sexual frustrations. "To read the list of books 'Banned in Boston' is to be shocked, not by the content of the books, but by the festering disease of the minds that find evil in them. Such minds have all the stigmata of the sexual invalid," Bernard DeVoto, a member of the Harvard faculty, wrote.[67]

A Massachusetts legislator introduced a bill requiring all censors to "submit to the state Department of Public Health satisfactory evidence of normal sexual experience." The bill was a joke, but there was growing support among legislators to change the law. In 1930, they approved amendments that ended the prosecution of literary works.[68]

Three years later, on the evening of May 10, Nazi youth burned thousands of books in thirty-four university towns across Germany, sending a shudder through the civilized world. Coming only five months after Adolf Hitler ascended to power, the conflagrations symbolized a hatred for intellectual discourse that many saw as a precursor to a new war, and Americans were outraged. More than a hundred thousand people in New York and fifty thousand in Chicago marched in protest.

Seven months later, US District Court judge John M. Woolsey lifted the ban that prevented the publication of *Ulysses* in the United States. Woolsey acknowledged that there were many dirty words in *Ulysses*, but he insisted that they did not make it obscene: "[W]hen such a real artist in words, as Joyce undoubtedly is, seeks to draw a true picture of the lower middle class in a European city, ought it to be impossible for the American legally to see the picture?"[69]

Although the fight for free speech was still in its infancy, civil libertarians had acquired some influential allies and won important battles.

FREE SPEECH REVOLUTION

In 1935, a ten-year-old boy and his eleven-year-old sister did a very brave thing in a small town in Pennsylvania coal country. They were Jehovah's Witnesses who had recently heard the leader of their church praise Witnesses in Germany for refusing to give the Nazi salute, which they considered a form of idolatry. As a result, the Nazis were putting them in concentration camps. More than one-third of them would die there.

William and Lillian Gobitas wanted to express solidarity with their German brothers and sisters. They decided they would refuse to perform a similarly idolatrous ritual, saluting the American flag during the Pledge of Allegiance, which started the school day.

On the day that the children had chosen to start their protest, Lillian's courage failed her. "I was very chicken," she said later. She was a straight-A student and president of her seventh-grade class. Lillian worried that she was about to lose her popularity. "Oh, if I stop saluting the flag I will blow all this," she told herself.[1]

Her younger brother William acted first, keeping his hand jammed into the pocket of his pants despite his teacher's best effort to pry it loose and force it into a salute. Lillian joined the boycott the next day. School officials expelled both children.

Jehovah's Witnesses were not popular in eastern Pennsylvania, or in many other American communities for that matter. They believed in the imminent arrival of Armageddon, and they pushed it hard in door-to-door proselytizing that many people found offensive. It did not help that the Witnesses arrogantly condemned other religions as "rackets." They were particularly hard on the Catholic Church, which they condemned as "the wickedest organization of liars, murderers and gangsters that has ever cursed the planet."

Lillian began "witnessing" at the age of eight, handing "testimony cards" to homeowners whom she had caught at home on a Sunday. "I have an important message," she told them. "Would you please read this?" Sometimes people were more than annoyed. Lillian was with a group of Jehovah's Witnesses when a mob attacked them in New Philadelphia, Pennsylvania.[2]

Nevertheless, two lower courts declared that the expulsion of William and Lillian violated their First Amendment rights. The Gobitas family was hopeful that the Supreme Court would agree. However, by the time the case finally reached the high court in the spring of 1940, a lot had changed. Another war had broken out in Europe, and there was once again a growing fear of extremism in the United States. The American Communist Party was small, but its membership had more than doubled to eighty thousand in just two years.

Admirers of Adolf Hitler and Benito Mussolini were also busy organizing groups. Although the number of domestic fascists was small, organizations like the Silver Shirts and the German American Bund attracted a lot of attention by dressing like Nazis and staging large demonstrations in New York, Cleveland, and Chicago.

The House of Representatives had created a special Committee on Un-American Activities in 1938 to investigate "the extent, character and objects of un-American propaganda activities in the United States." In 1940, Congress gave the president the nation's first peacetime anti-sedition act since 1798, making it a crime to "advocate, abet, advise, or teach the duty, necessity, desirability or propriety of overthrowing or destroying any government in the United States by force or violence."

Responding to the threat of internal subversion, the Supreme Court upheld the expulsion of the Gobitas children. In his majority opinion, Justice Felix Frankfurter declared that legislatures can pass laws to encourage the national unity even when they conflict with freedom of religion.

The *Minersville School District v. Gobitis* (*sic*; due to a clerical error, the Gobitas family name will forever be misspelled in the annals of American jurisprudence) case tainted the loyalty of the Witnesses at a dangerous time, and the reaction was immediate and terrifying. Mob violence swept the nation as Witnesses were "beaten, kidnapped, tarred and feathered, throttled in castor oil, tied together and chased through the streets, castrated, maimed, hanged, shot, and otherwise consigned to mayhem."[3]

Appeals to the police for protection were unavailing. In one Southern community, the sheriff watched as a mob assaulted seven Witnesses and hit a woman in the back with a brick. When an observer urged the sheriff to intervene, he refused. "They're traitors — the Supreme Court says so," he explained. In the three months following the *Gobitis* decision, the ACLU counted 236 attacks involving more than a thousand Witnesses in forty-four states.[4]

When the United States finally entered the war following the Japanese attack on Pearl Harbor on December 7, 1941, civil libertarians were hoping to avoid the kind of civil liberties meltdown that occurred during World War I. However, two months later President Franklin D. Roosevelt signed an executive order authorizing the forcible removal of 120,000 Japanese American citizens from their homes on the West Coast. The government sent them to ten hastily assembled prison camps in remote locations throughout the West.

The imprisonment of almost all of the country's citizens of Japanese ancestry, which occurred without a single documented case of treasonable conduct, is one of the worst violations of civil liberties in American history. During the war, the government also undertook more than two hundred prosecutions to punish individuals and groups based more on what they said than what they did. Nevertheless, there were fewer abuses of civil liberties during

World War II than there had been during World War I. This was mostly because there was no significant anti-war movement to generate the kind of dissent that occurred in 1917. In addition, the Justice Department worked actively to prevent state and local governments from embarking on another loyalty campaign. Attorney General Frances Biddle was an ACLU member.

There was also a remarkable change in the attitude of the Supreme Court. In 1942, three justices shocked the country by announcing that they had changed their minds and now believed that the First Amendment protected the right of Jehovah's Witnesses to refuse to salute the flag. Just three years after the decision in the *Gobitis* case, they acknowledged that "we now believe that it was wrongly decided." A year later, the Supreme Court overturned a regulation issued by the West Virginia Board of Education requiring students to salute the flag. It declared: "If there is any fixed star in our constitutional constellation, it is that no official, high or petty, can prescribe what shall be orthodox in politics, nationalism, religion or other matters of opinion or force citizens to confess by word or act their faith therein."[5]

Civil libertarians emerged from World War II confident that they were winning their fight for individual rights. The ACLU was clearly focused on the future as it announced that five of its eight "immediate tasks" involved an attack on racial discrimination.

However, the base of support for civil liberties was dangerously narrow. With only seven thousand members, the ACLU remained an organization that drew its support from a small segment of the upper middle class. What would happen if suddenly the government turned against it, and some of its strongest members dropped out? Nobody was asking this question in 1945. Yet the organization was about to face a new Red Scare that would last for nearly a decade, wiping away many of the gains that had been made since 1920.

It is understandable why the civil libertarians felt confident.

After all, the fascists had been defeated, and the world was safe for democracy. But there was another way to view foreign affairs that produced a far more pessimistic outlook.

The Soviet Union played a critical role in defeating Germany. After absorbing a Nazi invasion that cost the lives of millions, it launched a counterattack that drove to the doors of Hitler's bunker in Berlin, giving it vast new territories in the heart of Europe. Winston Churchill, Britain's wartime leader, expressed alarm that "an Iron Curtain had descended across the continent." Communism was spreading in other parts of the world as well. Communists took control of China in the summer of 1949.

Less than a year later, North Korean troops poured across the border of South Korea in an effort to unify the country under Communist rule. When the United Nations called on its members to support South Korea, Truman ordered US troops to intervene. America was at war again.

The threats from abroad focused attention on the danger of subversion at home. Evidence of Soviet spying began to appear soon after World War II ended. In 1945, Elizabeth Bentley, a thirty-seven-year-old Vassar graduate, told the FBI that dozens of federal employees in Washington had given her documents that she had passed to the Soviets.

Bentley created a national sensation when she testified before the House Un-American Activities Committee (HUAC). HUAC's next witness, Whittaker Chambers, caused even more widespread fear when he claimed that he, too, had been a Soviet courier and named Alger Hiss, who had served as a senior State Department official, as one of the spies in his network.

The evidence of spying by Communists suggested that there were American citizens, high-level government employees included, who would betray their country's deepest secrets. Wisconsin senator Joseph McCarthy charged that fifty-seven employees of the State Department were members of the Communist Party. The arrest of Julius and Ethel Rosenberg, who were accused of transmitting information that helped the Russians build an atomic bomb, seemed to confirm danger of Communist subversion.

Confronting a new Red Scare, the federal government once again responded by launching a sweeping attack on Communism that ruined the lives of thousands of people who were guilty of nothing more than having radical or even liberal ideas.

Under pressure from Republicans to oust Communists from government service, President Harry Truman launched a loyalty program that applied to all government employees, not just to those whose jobs could affect national security. It also involved investigating people who had done nothing to indicate disloyalty.

Investigators attempted to ferret out anyone found to belong to or have any "sympathetic association" with any "fascist, communist or subversive" groups. In practice, this meant any evidence of radical views, from the books people read to the paintings they hung on the walls of their homes.

The government fired people merely for associating with others who had radical ties. One man lost his job because his parents had an insurance policy issued by a company accused of being a Communist front. The most damning evidence often came from the FBI, which refused to reveal the sources of its information. Unable to confront their accusers, at least twelve thousand federal employees resigned as soon as they learned that they had failed their initial security screening.

The government also struck directly at the American Communist Party. Lacking any proof of criminal acts, it convicted eleven party leaders of a conspiracy to "advocate, abet, advise or teach the duty . . . of overthrowing or destroying any government in the United States by force." A judge sentenced them to ten years in prison.

HUAC held hearings on alleged subversion in the motion picture industry in an attempt to force people to admit they were Communists and identify other party members. When nine screenwriters and a director cited the First Amendment as grounds for refusing to answer, they were convicted of contempt and sent to jail for one year.

The Hollywood 10 were the first names on an unofficial blacklist that was used to deny employment in the movie industry. It grew to include two hundred screenwriters, actors, and directors who refused to cooperate with HUAC. Executives in the radio and TV industries bent to the demands of the Red baiters by refusing to hire anyone whose name was published in *Red Channels*, a periodical that accused more than 150 performers of radical connections.

The TV producer David Susskind reported that during a two-year period, loyalty screeners rejected more than fifteen hundred of the people he wanted to hire. Susskind said that they had even rejected an eight-year-old actress because her father was suspect.

State and local officials joined in the hunt for Communists. Almost every state and many local governments passed legislation that sought to weed out Communists on the public payroll. Some states followed the federal government in establishing loyalty reviews; others discharged employees who refused to take a loyalty oath.

Colleges and universities fired at least one hundred professors for their political views. There were probably many more. Hundreds of elementary and secondary school teachers were also dismissed. The New York City Board of Education fired three hundred teachers on political grounds.

The new Red Scare should have been the ACLU's shining hour. At times, it fought brilliantly, including publishing an exposé of the Hollywood blacklist. However, the leaders of the ACLU often disagreed over how to respond.

In 1940, under pressure from HUAC, the ACLU board passed a resolution barring Communists and other members of "totalitarian" groups from serving as board members. It also expelled Elizabeth Gurley Flynn, the former Wobblie. She had joined the Communist Party and served on its national committee.

On several issues, the ACLU supported greater restrictions on free speech. It refused to help the singer Paul Robeson when the State Department revoked his passport in 1950. Robeson was a strong critic of America's racial policies and a defender of the Soviet Union. That was enough to persuade many that he was an enemy of America. There was a riot when he attempted to perform in Peekskill, New York.

The government revoked Robeson's passport because he refused to sign an affidavit denying that he was a Communist. Already blacklisted in the United States, he found it virtually impossible to make a living abroad after the revocation. The ACLU did not challenge the government's claim that the First Amendment does not guarantee an unrestricted right to travel.

When even the ACLU was afraid to take an uncompromising stand in defense of civil liberties, it is not surprising that support for free speech among the public sank to a new low in the early 1950s. A reporter for a Wisconsin newspaper proved this by creating a petition that included nothing but the preamble to the Declaration of Independence. Only 1 percent of the people he approached agreed to sign.

"Fear has driven more and more men and women in all walks of life either to silence or to the folds of the orthodox," Supreme Court justice William O. Douglas wrote in 1952.[6]

"Ideas Can Be Dangerous"

Despite facing many obstacles, librarians, surprisingly, would emerge as leading defenders of free expression during this time. The library profession was not as prestigious as most other careers. The typical male librarian was "rather submissive in social situations and less likely [than the average college student] to show qualities of leadership," a 1952 study reported.[7]

The fact that most of the country's more than thirty thousand librarians worked for public institutions and were therefore accountable at some point to elected politicians encouraged them to censor controversial books. "I have never met a public librarian who approved of censorship or one who failed to practice it in some measure," a library school professor observed.[8]

However, a handful of people were strong advocates for the view that protecting free speech was a critical part of the librarian's professional responsibilities. In 1939, the American Library Association had adopted the Library's Bill of Rights. Pointing to the "growing intolerance, suppression of free speech and censorship" abroad, the ALA had declared that librarians should purchase books based on their "value and interest" and should ignore "the race or nationality or the political or religious views of the writers." In addition, libraries should try to present all sides of controversial issues and make their meeting rooms available "to all groups in the community regardless of their beliefs or affiliations."[9]

Even before the ink was dry on the Library's Bill of Rights, controversy erupted over John Steinbeck's new novel, *The Grapes of Wrath*. *Collier's* magazine condemned its portrait of the mistreatment of migrant workers as "propaganda for the idea that we ought to change our system for the Russian system."[10]

In response to this outcry, the Kansas City, Missouri, Board of Education banned the book from school library shelves. Libraries around the country joined in the ban, although at least one librarian attempted to salve his conscience by denying that he had censored the book — he had merely refused to buy it.

The ALA created the Special Committee on Censorship to determine what steps it could take to help librarians live up to their Bill of Rights. Educating librarians was obviously a priority. The committee would have to "awaken" librarians to "the principle of freedom," a librarian at the University of California at Berkeley declared. In 1940, the special committee became permanent and was renamed the Committee on Intellectual Freedom to Safeguard the Rights of

Library Users to Freedom of Inquiry. A few years later, it shortened its name to the Intellectual Freedom Committee (IFC).[11]

After World War II, the IFC pushed ALA into the forefront of the censorship fight against the American Legion, the Daughters of the American Revolution, and other patriotic groups who were pressuring libraries to purge their collections of "un-American" materials. It called for a strengthening of the Library's Bill of Rights, which did not explicitly state that fighting censorship was a duty of all librarians.

The new statement, adopted in 1948, expressed the new imperative plainly: "Censorship of books, urged or practiced by volunteer arbiters of morals or political opinion or by organizations that would establish a coercive concept of Americans, must be challenged by libraries."[12]

The ALA demonstrated its new militancy by opposing the New York City Board of Education's banning of *The Nation* magazine. It also helped defeat a plan to appoint a censorship board in Los Angeles County. (A member of the board of supervisors had accused the chief librarian of possessing "those liberal thoughts that we don't like in the mind of the head of our library.")[13]

Still, most librarians remained skeptical of the ALA's aggressive new policy on censorship. Many state library associations resisted the call to form their own intellectual freedom committees, preferring to let sleeping dogs lie.

This complacency received a severe shock in 1950 when the library board in Bartlesville, Oklahoma, fired Ruth Brown, an employee with thirty years of service. The board was angry because she had challenged racial segregation by accompanying two Black friends to a whites-only restaurant and requesting service.

Its members chose to make an issue of Brown's purchase for the library of subscriptions to five "subversive" publications — *The Nation, New Republic, Soviet Russia Today, Negro Digest,* and *Consumer Reports.* "What do you think of buying such trash from your very inadequate book fund?" a commissioner asked during a hearing, referring to *The Nation* and *New Republic*.[14]

Ruth Brown's case riveted the attention of other librarians. If Brown could be fired for subscribing to mainstream magazines, then no librarian's job was safe. Ten years later, an ALA journal declared that the Ruth Brown case did more "than any other in our time to shock librarians into examining their beliefs in intellectual freedom."[15]

The support for free speech among librarians increased after attacks by Joseph McCarthy and his supporters.

Following the outbreak of the Korean War, the American Legion in Peoria, Illinois, demanded that the local library withdraw from circulation several films that it said contained Communist propaganda. In Montclair, New Jersey, the Sons of the American Revolution wanted the library to label and restrict the circulation of all "Communistic or subversive" books and magazines. They also asked the librarian to keep a record of everyone who used the labeled material.

The ALA took a strong stand against labeling as "an attempt to prejudice the reader, and as such, it is a censor's tool," but it was powerless when McCarthy himself led the campaign to censor government libraries abroad. He claimed that libraries operated by the State Department included books written by un-American authors.[16]

The government responded by banning material by "any controversial persons, Communists, fellow travelers, 'et cetera.'" It went on to issue a blizzard of directives, requiring the removal of specific issues of periodicals that contained material deemed harmful to American interests, including an issue of the *Annals of the American Academy of Political and Social Science* that contained an article about the United Nations, a frequent target of conservatives.

The threat of McCarthyism convinced the leaders of the ALA to seek support from outside of the library community.

Over a weekend in early May 1953, twenty-five librarians, book publishers, and citizens "representing the public interest" met at the Westchester Country Club in Rye, New York, to discuss how to halt what the IFC chair called the "national trend toward the restriction of the free trade in ideas."[7]

The result was *The Freedom to Read*, a statement that its drafters urged the ALA and the American Book Publishers Council to adopt. "The freedom to read is essential to our democracy. It is under attack," the statement began. "We, as citizens devoted to the use of books and as librarians and publishers responsible for disseminating them, wish to assert the public interest in the preservation of the freedom to read."[8]

The statement identified specific propositions defining the freedom to read:

- It was in the public interest for publishers and librarians to make available the widest diversity of views and expressions.

- Publishers and librarians do not need to endorse every idea or presentation contained in the books they make available.

- A book should be judged by its content, not the political views of its author.

- While obscenity laws must be enforced, it is wrong to limit the efforts of writers to achieve their artistic goals and to deny to adults books that may be unsuitable for adolescents.

Finally, the statement pledged that librarians and publishers, "as guardians of the people's freedom," would "contest encroachments upon that freedom by individuals or groups seeking to impose their own standards or tastes upon the community at large."

"We do not state these propositions in the comfortable belief that what people read is unimportant," the statement concluded. "We believe rather that what people read is deeply important; that ideas can be dangerous; but that the suppression of ideas is fatal to a democratic society. Freedom itself is a dangerous way of life, but it is ours."

Despite the statement's eloquence, there was no guarantee that the ALA annual conference would adopt it.

Then, just a week before the ALA meeting, President Dwight Eisenhower, who had assiduously avoided criticizing McCarthy, shocked many by condemning censorship in a speech at Dartmouth College's commencement. "Don't join the book burners," Eisenhower said. "Don't be afraid to go in your library and read every book as long as any document does not offend our own ideas of decency. That should be the only censorship."[19]

The president's words electrified the librarians, and they arrived at their annual conference eager to approve *The Freedom to Read*. When the moment came, the statement was endorsed "overwhelmingly by a shouting and enthusiastic vote."[20]

A large section of the press hailed it as well. *The New York Times* ranked the statement with "America's outstanding state papers" and joined *The Washington Post*, *The Christian Science Monitor*, and *The Baltimore Sun* in reprinting it in full.

The American Booksellers Association, the American Newspaper Guild, and the American Bar Association quickly announced their support.

After six years on the defensive, liberals were beginning to assert themselves again. In the fall of 1953, just a few months after the publication of *The Freedom to Read*, the Supreme Court got a new chief justice. Earl Warren, a Republican who had served three terms as governor of California, believed that the Supreme Court should play an active role in the political process, correcting injustices that the legislative and executive branches refused to address.

In 1954, the Supreme Court unanimously repudiated its 1897

decision in *Plessy v. Ferguson* that had upheld the constitutionality of segregation. In *Brown v. Board of Education*, it ordered the Topeka, Kansas, schools to integrate with "all deliberate speed."

Several years later, the Warren court began to undo the damage to civil liberties that had occurred during the Red Scare. On the same day in 1957, the justices issued decisions in four cases that struck at different aspects of the anti-Communist program.

In the most important case, Justice John M. Harlan drew a clear line between criminal conduct and protected speech. The "essential distinction is that those to whom the advocacy is addressed must be urged to *do* something, now or in the future, rather than merely to *believe* in something," he wrote in a majority opinion.[21]

Booksellers, publishers, and even movie distributors began turning to the courts to find some relief from censorship.

In 1957, US customs agents decided that *Howl*, a book of poems by Allen Ginsberg, was obscene and seized five hundred copies that its publisher had printed abroad. Later, San Francisco police purchased a copy of the book from a clerk at the City Lights Bookstore. They charged both the clerk, Shigeyoshi Murao, and Lawrence Ferlinghetti, the bookstore owner and the publisher of *Howl*, with selling an obscene book.

At that moment, the Supreme Court was deciding the case of *Roth v. US*, which would determine whether the Comstock obscenity law would continue to determine what Americans could read almost a century later. Samuel Roth had been convicted under a federal statute criminalizing the sending of "obscene, lewd, lascivious or filthy" materials through the mail for selling *American Aphrodite*, a publication that contained nude photos and erotica.

Warren assigned the task of writing the majority opinion to another recent appointee to the court, William J. Brennan Jr., who had previously served on the New Jersey Supreme Court. Brennan was not a free speech absolutist. He did not believe that the First Amendment protected obscenity, and he joined five other members of the court in sustaining the conviction of Samuel Roth.

However, Brennan's opinion endorsed an updated and more permissive definition of obscenity. "[S]ex and obscenity are not synonymous," he wrote, finding that the First Amendment protected any work with sexual content that is not "utterly without redeeming social importance." At first, supporters of obscenity laws saw the decision to affirm Roth's conviction as a victory. Then the Supreme Court began issuing rulings that demonstrated that Comstock's law was dead.[22]

Publishers were soon testing the limits of the Supreme Court's new tolerance for works with sexual content. In 1958, G. P. Putnam published Vladimir Nabokov's *Lolita*, the story of a man's sexual relationship with a twelve-year-old girl.

When prosecutors decided not to challenge *Lolita*, an iconoclastic publisher, Barney Rosset, was emboldened to publish an unexpurgated paperback of one of the most notorious books in the English language, *Lady Chatterley's Lover*. The postal authorities who had long enforced Comstock's law tried to have the book declared obscene, but a federal judge ruled against them, citing the *Roth* decision.

New York Times v. Sullivan

The Supreme Court decisions of the 1950s protected the rights of radicals and began to limit book and movie censorship in the United States. Arguably, these changes affected relatively few people. However, a battle had begun that would have a profound influence on the First Amendment rights of all Americans.

In December 1955, police arrested Rosa Parks, a Black activist in Montgomery, Alabama, for refusing to move from the whites-only section of a municipal bus. The Black community responded by launching a boycott of the bus system. Martin Luther King

Jr., a twenty-six-year-old minister who had recently moved to Alabama, took command on the first day of the boycott by delivering a powerful speech to people in the Dexter Avenue Baptist Church and thousands listening outside.

King declared that the Black citizens of Montgomery were rebelling against oppression, but they had no desire for blood. "Now let us say that we are not here advocating violence," King said. "The only weapon that we have in our hands this evening is the weapon of protest. If we were incarcerated behind the iron curtains of a communistic nation — we couldn't do this. If we were trapped in the dungeon of a totalitarian regime — we couldn't do this. But the great glory of American democracy is the right to protest for the right."[23]

King knew that many would criticize the bus boycott as a form of coercion. But he insisted that the use of nonviolent force was a legitimate form of protest. "Not only are we using the tools of persuasion — but we've got to use the tools of coercion," he said.[24]

It was the start of a titanic struggle.

The Supreme Court's decision a year earlier in *Brown v. Board of Education*, ordering an end to segregation in public schools, had stunned white southerners. For a moment, it seemed that they might peacefully accept the end of segregation. However, opponents of the decision were soon organizing at the local level. White Citizens' Councils dedicated to "states' rights" and "racial integrity" enrolled 250,000 members in hundreds of communities throughout the South over the next two years.

By that time, southern members of Congress had found their voice. "We regard the decision of the Supreme Court in the school cases as a clear abuse of judicial power," 101 of the 128 southern members of the House and Senate declared in a "Southern Manifesto." "We pledge ourselves to use all lawful means to reverse [it]."[25]

Virginia senator Harry F. Byrd promised "massive resistance" to *Brown*. Soon White Citizens' Councils began targeting any southerner who seemed willing to compromise on the issue of race.

In Little Rock, Arkansas, where federal troops had to protect the nine Black students who desegregated Central High School, the Capitol Citizens' Council organized economic boycotts against defenders of integration, including the *Arkansas Gazette*, which lost 10 percent of its circulation. It boycotted a baker because his teenage daughter was known to oppose segregation and one of his employees was a member of the school board that approved the integration of the high school.

The Ku Klux Klan reemerged and attempted to intimidate those who could not be persuaded by lawful means.

Despite their anger at the Supreme Court, the segregationists' main nemesis was not the federal government but a private organization — the National Association for the Advancement of Colored People (NAACP). At a time when the federal government remained unwilling to play an active role in securing equal rights for African Americans, the NAACP had taken the lead in forcing the issue of race onto the national agenda. The NAACP took the school segregation issue to the Supreme Court.

Only a small fraction of the NAACP's three hundred thousand members lived in the South. There were only fourteen thousand NAACP members in the entire state of Alabama — and almost all of them were Black. What they lacked in numbers, they made up for in bravery. In the wake of the *Brown* decision, they began to file petitions urging their local school boards to comply with the Supreme Court's order that schools desegregate "with all deliberate speed."

The segregationists did not have to depend only upon terror to turn back these challenges to the racial status quo. As the "Southern Manifesto" demonstrated, they had the support of the region's political leaders, and they used their control of the South's political institutions to conduct a systematic campaign to suppress the protest — legally.

Police arrested King and a hundred others on a charge of conducting an illegal conspiracy in connection with the three-month-old bus boycott. Just a month later, King was convicted and ordered to pay a $500 fine or spend 386 days in jail. He refused to pay.

Soon after King's conviction, the Alabama attorney general sued the NAACP, accusing it of engaging in injurious activities by supporting the bus boycott and furnishing legal assistance to Black students who were trying to enroll in the state university.

Reviving the tactic of exposure that had been used against the Klan in 1923 and against the Communists in 1950, the attorney general obtained an injunction barring further NAACP activity in Alabama until the organization provided a list of the names of all of its members in the state. The NAACP refused to turn over the list because it knew that segregationists would use it to threaten its members with economic reprisals and "actual force." Unmoved, the judge hit the organization with a $100,000 fine for contempt.

Southern legislators enthusiastically embraced the idea of exposing the NAACP's membership, convinced that the racial unrest that was sweeping the South was the result of outside agitators stirring up trouble among otherwise contented folk. Virginia and four other states introduced legislation targeting membership records. The Virginia legislature also attempted to prevent NAACP lawyers from bringing legal challenges to racial discrimination by making it illegal for them to seek clients.

Other states tried different approaches. The Arkansas legislature banned the hiring of NAACP members by any state or local government agency, including school boards. The ban's author, Arkansas attorney general Bruce Bennett, proclaimed that it "was meant to harass and cripple the NAACP and as such has accomplished its purpose."26

However, the US Supreme Court would have the final say on the constitutionality of anti-NAACP legislation. No fewer than six cases reached the court between 1957 and 1965, and the justices made their position very clear.

The first important case to come before the court involved Alabama's effort to force the NAACP to turn over its membership list. Writing for a unanimous court, Justice John M. Harlan reversed the judgment against the NAACP, voiding the $100,000 fine for contempt. Harlan wrote that it clearly violated the right to associate with others to advocate political views.

The Supreme Court also swept aside Virginia's effort to curb NAACP litigation. In his majority opinion, Justice Brennan broke new constitutional ground by declaring for the first time that litigation is a form of speech and, therefore, protected by the First Amendment.

An even broader affirmation of First Amendment rights was on the horizon.

In February 1960, four Black students sat down at a whites-only lunch counter in Greensboro, North Carolina, and refused to leave when they were denied service. Students throughout the South followed their example. State colleges had them arrested and later expelled some.

To raise funds to defend the protesters, the Committee to Defend Martin Luther King and the Struggle for Freedom in the South published a full-page ad in *The New York Times* that described efforts to suppress the civil rights movement. Titled "Heed Their Rising Voices," it included details of police abuse of students at the state college in Montgomery, Alabama.

L. B. Sullivan, a county commissioner who was in charge of the Montgomery police, seized on a number of minor factual errors in the ad to claim the *Times* had libeled him and damaged his reputation. His lawsuit demanded $500,000, a sum that was daunting even for a newspaper as large as the *Times*. Other politicians quickly piled on. Soon eleven Alabama officials were demanding that the *Times* pay more than $5 million.

The newspaper was in trouble. Libel laws favored the plaintiff. Sullivan did not have to show any evidence of damage to his reputation. The newspaper would have only one defense — truth — and several of the statements had been false.

Sullivan had filed his lawsuit in an Alabama state court, and the judge assigned to the case had issued decisions restricting the NAACP, enjoining civil rights demonstrations, and blocking the Justice Department from examining voting records. *Times* executives expected no mercy, and they received none. At the end of a three-day trial, the judge ordered them to pay Sullivan $500,000.

The *Times* faced a dilemma. Although it was one of the country's premiere publications, it was not highly profitable, and the Alabama lawsuits threatened its survival. There seemed little hope that it would prevail by appealing to the Alabama Supreme Court or even the US Supreme Court. The right to sue for libel had existed for centuries in both English and American law.

The leaders of the *Times* were seriously considering not appealing when Herbert Wechsler, the lawyer representing the newspaper, convinced them that they had a chance. He explained that the Supreme Court had been expanding the First Amendment and urged them to break new constitutional ground by arguing that some libelous statements might be protected speech.

Wechsler believed that the court would be willing to take a fresh look at libel law if it found the right case. The *Sullivan* case threatened to restrict reporting on a matter of national concern. This could be the right case, he said, and he was right.

The Supreme Court justices were unanimous in overturning the libel award. In writing the high court's opinion, Justice Brennan avoided any mention of recent events. Instead, he recalled the history of the Sedition Act of 1798 to prove that the right to criticize government was "the central meaning of the First Amendment."

Brennan quoted James Madison, the author of the Bill of Rights and a leader of the fight against the Sedition Act. "The people, not the government, possesses the absolute sovereignty," Madison wrote in his *Report on the Virginia Resolutions*. It followed, Brennan observed, that "free public discussion of the stewardship of public officials" is a "fundamental principle of American government."[27]

Brennan wrote: "[W]e consider this case against the background of a profound national commitment to the principle that debate on public issues should be uninhibited, robust, and wide-open, and that it may well include vehement, caustic and sometimes unpleasantly sharp attacks on government and public officials."

To make possible such passionate debate, it was necessary to create "breathing room" for errors of fact, Brennan declared. Again, he quoted Madison: "Some degree of abuse is inseparable from the proper use of everything; and in no instance is this more true than in that of the press."

Brennan declared that the only punishable criticisms of public officials are those made with "actual malice" — statements made with knowledge that they are false or with reckless disregard of the facts indicating whether they were true.

The decision in *New York Times v. Sullivan* case was an enormous step forward in the effort to protect the free speech rights of individuals as well as the press. It shifted the burden of proof in libel cases from defendants, who were no longer required to show that everything they had said or written was true, to public officials, who had to demonstrate that defendants knowingly or recklessly made false statements.

As a result, it freed dissenters and critics from a fear of retaliation by angry public officials. This freedom would be of great importance in the coming years when opponents of the war in Vietnam bitterly criticized the government.

The importance of the decision was already clear to First Amendment scholars. "It is an occasion for dancing in the street," one said.[28]

Civil Rights, Vietnam, Watergate:
The Right to Protest and the Right to Know

The civil rights movement had used every form of protest to make its point: boycotts, picketing, sit-ins, marches, rallies, and even paid newspaper advertisements, which were now protected by the First Amendment, thanks to the *Sullivan* decision.

The example of thousands of men, women, and children fighting for equal rights at the risk of their lives inspired admiration throughout the country, and no more so than among the students who were flooding the nation's colleges and universities following the postwar baby boom.

Students in the North organized demonstrations of their own. In San Francisco, students from the University of California at Berkeley sat down in the lobby of the Sheraton Palace Hotel in a successful effort to force the hiring of more Black employees. Others picketed branches of the chain stores that were the targets of sit-in demonstrations in the South. The bravest students went South themselves, joining the Freedom Ride in 1961, which challenged the segregation of interstate travel and participating in the effort to register Black voters during the Freedom Summer of 1964.

Racists frequently attacked the northerners. In the same summer as the *Sullivan* decision, Michael Schwerner and Andrew Goodman, two white civil rights workers from New York, and their colleague, James Chaney, an African American from Mississippi, were killed by the Ku Klux Klan.

Many of the students who went South were natural rebels like Tom Hayden. He began his career as an activist when he entered the University of Michigan in 1957 and discovered that it denied students basic rights. He was appalled when the university expelled several students for allegedly throwing food at a housemother during a fracas in the dormitory cafeteria. The incident had begun as a protest over a requirement that men wear dress shirts and ties.

The university dismissed the students without a hearing. "It was a system of absolute arbitrary authority," Hayden recalled.[29]

Hayden soon began to focus on larger problems — civil rights, the very hot Cold War with its threat of instant annihilation, and the rise of a mass society that appeared to crush individualism and undermine democracy.

He met other students who shared his view that radical action was necessary. Some of them were the children of left-wing parents, but students of all political backgrounds were showing a new interest in politics. At its 1960 convention, the National Student Association declared that the role of the student "involves a commitment to an education process that extends beyond classroom training. It involves also the attainment of knowledge and the development of skills and habits of mind and action necessary for responsible participation in the affairs of government and society on all levels — campus, community, state, national, international."[30]

Hayden and a small group of students went further. They believed that students could be a force for social change. In 1962, they gave full voice to this belief at a convention of the Students for a Democratic Society (SDS). In *The Port Huron Statement*, a sixty-three-page manifesto drafted by Hayden, SDS called for the birth of a "participatory democracy" that would make it possible for every individual to achieve independence and find "a meaning in life that is personally authentic." One participant recalled, "It felt like the dawn of a new age."[31]

SDS's dream of a national reform movement driven by students appeared to be coming true. The year before students at the all-black Alabama State College had won an important legal victory when a federal appeals court ruled that college officials had violated their rights by expelling them for participating in a sit-in.

In 1964, students at the University of California at Berkeley responded with outrage when the university ordered them to stop distributing political literature on university property. Suspecting the administration of attempting to curb their efforts to pressure local employers to hire more Blacks, they joined with conservative students who wanted to be politically active to launch a free speech movement.

The organizers of the protest announced that they would oppose the restrictions on their speech by bringing the tactics of the civil rights movement to the Berkeley campus. Administrators got their first taste of southern protest when they attempted to arrest Jack Weinberg, a civil rights worker who had set up a literature table directly in front of the administration building, Sproul Hall. As the police grabbed him, Weinberg went limp, forcing the officers to carry him through an excited crowd of two to three hundred students.

Someone yelled, "Sit down!" The crowd instantly obeyed, and the police found themselves and their patrol car surrounded. Soon thousands of students were crowding around to see what was happening and sitting down to join the protest.

A twenty-two-year-old transfer student, Mario Savio, asked if he could address the students from the top of the car. A policeman told him to remove his shoes. There, in white socks, Savio emerged as the leader of the student protest. Savio was a Catholic who shared the liberal views of the Catholic Worker Movement and liberation theology. He was also a veteran of the Freedom Summer.

"We were going to hold a rally," Savio told the crowd. "We didn't know how to get the people. But we've got them now thanks to the University." Later, he met with administrators and negotiated a truce that ended a thirty-hour standoff, releasing both Weinberg and the patrol car.[32]

Over the next two months, Savio and his supporters would repeatedly provoke the administration into overreaction. They occupied Sproul Hall, which led to the arrest of eight hundred students. Later, police seized Savio and dragged him away as he attempted to speak at an event sponsored by the university,

Mario Savio atop a police car at the University of California, Berkeley, 1964

Savio's arrest galvanized faculty members, who voted 824–115 to support the free speech movement. "I kept pinching myself that this place was real," one of the protesters recalled. "The world seemed deeply good." A week later, the administration capitulated, granting the students all the rights guaranteed by the First Amendment.[33]

At the start of 1965, there seemed to be every reason to be optimistic about the prospects for social change. The assassination of President John F. Kennedy in the fall of 1963 had traumatized the nation, but the new president, Lyndon Johnson of Texas, rejected the reactionary leadership of the South and broke a filibuster to pass the Civil Rights Act of 1964.

A shadow hung over the dreams for the future, however. Johnson was steadily escalating American involvement in the civil war between North and South Vietnam. By the end of 1966, nearly four hundred thousand American soldiers were fighting in Southeast Asia.

Opposition to the war grew quickly. Many of the leaders of the student movement felt sympathy for the national liberation movements around the world that were seeking to throw off the corrupt and anti-democratic regimes that had been installed by colonial powers. Many protesters also had a personal reason for opposing the war: Men over the age of eighteen who were not attending college were subject to the military draft.

In 1965, the first protest occurred at the University of Michigan, where more than three thousand students and teachers participated in a "teach-in" on the war. The next month, SDS organizers were surprised when more than twenty thousand people turned out for a Washington demonstration.

Anti-war protesters immediately ran into opposition. The Senate Internal Security Committee claimed that the demonstrators were "communist and extremist elements who are openly sympathetic to the Vietcong and openly hostile to the United States."[34]

Supporters of the war tried to punish protesters. They pelted people marching in demonstration with eggs and paint and sometimes physically assaulted them. The Georgia House of Representatives refused to seat Julian Bond, a civil rights worker and pacifist who had criticized the war. In Des Moines, Iowa, school officials suspended John Tinker, fifteen, and his thirteen-year-old sister, Beth, for wearing black armbands protesting the war.

Johnson became convinced that only Russian manipulation could explain the growth of the anti-war movement. In 1967, he encouraged the Central Intelligence Agency to begin spying on dissenters in an effort to uncover their links to foreign agents. Under the leadership of J. Edgar Hoover, the FBI already had an expansive campaign in place for spying on American citizens. It had begun installing illegal wiretaps on the telephones of Communists at least as early as the 1940s, and probably even earlier. The FBI also planted secret microphones and conducted break-ins with such regularity that they had their own name: "black bag jobs," for the bag that held the burglar tools.

When the FBI was occasionally caught in illegal acts, its spokesmen argued that the agents were engaged in intelligence gathering that was necessary to protect the nation's security. But the purpose of the spying was broader than that. It was a tactic in a clandestine war waged by Hoover's FBI against not just enemy spies but also the Communist Party of the United States of America (CPUSA) and other "subversive" groups that were considered suspicious mainly because of their opposition to the Red Scare.

The FBI's knowledge of the inside workings of dissident groups created an enormous temptation for Hoover and his agents to intervene directly in their affairs and attempt to disrupt them. FBI informants were often in a position to spread lies that would cause internal dissension, sometimes by raising suspicion about the loyalty of key leaders.

In 1956, as it became apparent that the Supreme Court was intent on expanding protections for civil liberties that would make it harder to convict Communists, Hoover ordered the launch of a full-blown counterintelligence program (COINTELPRO).

The program nearly succeeded in wiping out the CPUSA altogether as FBI agents and informants undertook nearly fourteen hundred actions intended to undermine the morale of their enemies. By the end of 1957, there were only 3,474 members left in the party.

Hoover was so impressed with the results of COINTELPRO that he turned it against other groups. In 1961, he targeted the Socialist Workers Party. In 1964, in response to the violence against civil rights workers in the South, he added the Ku Klux Klan and other white hate groups to the list. In 1967, the FBI began to pursue militant African American groups like the Black Panther Party. A year later, COINTELPRO began targeting radical opponents of the Vietnam War.

The FBI showed no ability to distinguish between dissenters and criminals. The most glaring example of this was its campaign to discredit Martin Luther King. When Hoover learned that one of the civil rights leader's closest advisers had been a high-ranking member of the Communist Party, he ordered King's telephone tapped and bugs planted in his hotel rooms. In the most notorious act of the COINTELPRO era, an assistant director of the FBI sent King an anonymous letter threatening to expose his extramarital affairs.

King was in Sweden accepting the Nobel Peace Prize when the letter arrived at the Southern Christian Leadership Council's office, accompanied by a recording of conversations and sounds of sexual activity taped in King's hotel rooms. Not suspecting what it was, King's wife, Coretta, opened the package and listened to the tape. She called her husband. "They are out to break me," King said. "They are out to get me, harass me, break my spirit."[35]

The FBI also worked actively to undermine the anti-war movement. In 1968, a directive went out from Washington to all bureau offices ordering them to "collect evidence on the 'scurrilous and depraved nature of many of the characters, activities, habits, and living conditions representative of New Left adherents.'" One tactic was to send anonymous letters about student misbehavior to parents, neighbors, and employers. In the days before the Democratic National Convention in Chicago in 1968, the FBI succeeded in disrupting plans for housing demonstrators.[36]

FBI agents undertook nearly a thousand actions against the Klan and the anti-war and civil rights movements.

The attacks on the anti-war movement might have been more successful if the Supreme Court had not steadfastly protected protest throughout the Vietnam War. The court ordered Georgia to allow Julian Bond to take his seat in the state legislature. It also upheld the right of John and Mary Beth Tinker to protest in school and overturned the conviction of Paul Robert Cohen for wearing a jacket that said FUCK THE DRAFT in the corridor of a California courthouse.

The Supreme Court demonstrated just how serious it was about protecting politically provocative speech when it unanimously overturned the conviction of a member of the Ku Klux Klan. He was accused of violating an Ohio law making it a crime to teach "the duty, necessity, or propriety of crime, sabotage, violence, or unlawful methods of terrorism as a means of accomplishing industrial or political reform."[37]

It ruled that advocating violence or other criminal acts alone was not adequate grounds for banning speech. The police can only intervene "where such advocacy is directed to inciting or producing imminent lawless action and is likely to produce such action." The "clear and present danger" test that Justices Holmes and Brandeis had advocated as a safeguard for free speech in 1919 had finally become the law of the land.[38]

One of the most important cases for the Supreme Court lay ahead. In 1971, *The New York Times* began publishing a secret government study of the Vietnam War known as the Pentagon Papers. When the Justice Department asked a judge to block the publication of further installments in the series, the Supreme Court faced one of its most difficult decisions. It would have to decide whether the government's interest in protecting national security was more important than free speech, and it would have to do it in the middle of a war.

The *Times* knew that the Pentagon Papers study was going to cause trouble. Secretary of Defense Robert McNamara had commissioned the study of American policy in Vietnam in the hope that it would identify the mistakes that had led the United States into a disastrous military intervention.

One of the authors, Daniel Ellsberg, a national security analyst who had become a passionate critic of the war, was convinced that the Pentagon Papers could end the war. Ellsberg tried to give documents he had secretly copied to anti-war leaders in Congress, but they were unwilling to accept responsibility for revealing classified information. Finally, he gave the study to Neil Sheehan, a *Times* reporter. Later, he also delivered it to *The Washington Post*.

The lawyers for the newspapers faced formidable obstacles as the trial opened in the federal courthouse in Manhattan. Nixon had just appointed the judge, Murray Gurfein. The Pentagon Papers case was his first.

The biggest challenge was the government's claim that the release of a forty-seven-volume report that included thousands of pages of classified documents would harm national security by damaging diplomatic relations, exposing intelligence operations, and providing the enemy with useful information about military planning.

Yet the government failed. Gurfein lifted his injunction the next day. The Supreme Court affirmed his decision two weeks later. Journalists and civil libertarians were jubilant over the 6–3 ruling because it recognized the importance of free speech even in time of war. The words of Judge Gurfein's decision made the point best: "The security of the Nation is not at the ramparts alone. Security also lies in the value of our free institutions. A cantankerous press, an obstinate press, a ubiquitous press must be suffered by those in authority in order to preserve the even greater values of freedom of expression and the right of the people to know."

When *The New York Times* and *The Washington Post* resumed publication of the Pentagon Papers, the revelations fueled a national debate over whether the government of the United States had tricked the American people into an unwinnable war. They also prompted President Richard Nixon to authorize the formation of an investigative unit within the White House and assigned it the job of cracking down on government leakers, starting with Daniel Ellsberg.

On June 17, 1972, the police arrested five members of the unit, known as the Plumbers, as they attempted to burglarize the offices of the Democratic National Committee in the Watergate building in Washington, DC. Two years of investigation by *The Washington Post*, Federal District Court judge John J. Sirica, and committees of the House and Senate revealed that high officials in the Nixon administration had approved the burglary.

Nixon himself had participated in covering up the payment of hush money to the burglars. In July 1974, the House Judiciary Committee approved three articles of impeachment. Nixon resigned just two years after he had won reelection in a landslide.

Almost before the country could breathe a sigh of relief over the end of the Watergate horrors, however, came more shocking revelations of government wrongdoing. *The New York Times* reported that the CIA had been engaged in a massive campaign of spying on American citizens. Although forbidden by law to operate in the United States, the CIA had used illegal break-ins, wiretaps, and mail openings to gather information on more than ten thousand anti-war protesters and other dissidents. The *Times* published thirty-two stories detailing the sins of the agency.

The Washington Post joined in describing the misdeeds of the secret government by revealing that the FBI had spied on members of Congress and collected information about their personal lives. It also exposed the first evidence of the plot to discredit Martin Luther King; and Daniel Schorr, a correspondent for the *CBS Evening News*, revealed that the CIA had participated in attempts to assassinate foreign leaders.

Congress worked quickly to follow up the charges made by the press. The Senate established a special committee headed by Frank Church of Idaho and charged it with describing the operations of the "shadow government" created by the intelligence agencies.

The Church Committee did not disappoint. The public hearings opened with the revelation that the CIA possessed shellfish toxin and cobra venom for use in assassination attempts. Later, the committee confirmed that the CIA had tried to kill Fidel Castro and African nationalist Patrice Lumumba. It also revealed many of the secrets of the COINTELPRO program, including the full story of the FBI's effort to blackmail King.

The Church Committee published its final report in six volumes in 1976. It revealed that the CIA had engaged in nine hundred covert actions since 1961; that its computers contained the names of 1.5 million potentially "subversive" Americans; and that it had spied on 7,000 of them. The CIA and FBI had opened 380,000 letters and had investigated more than five hundred thousand dissidents without proving that any of them were guilty of committing a crime.

The report recommended nearly two hundred changes in foreign and domestic intelligence gathering to eliminate the danger of further abuses of civil liberties.

Congress approved some of the most important reforms in November 1974, even before the country began to learn of the abuses committed by its intelligence agencies. These were a series of amendments to the Freedom of Information Act.

Harold L. Cross, a former counsel for the *New York Herald Tribune*, had launched a campaign to establish the public's right to gain access to government information in 1953. "Public business is the public's business," Cross declared in his book *The People's Right to Know*.[39]

Commissioned by the American Society of Newspaper Editors, Cross's book acknowledged that reporters were skilled at obtaining information from public officials. However, there were few laws that actually compelled the disclosure of public information when the officials turned obstinate.

When the Freedom of Information Act became law in 1966, it contained numerous exemptions and lacked important enforcement provisions. The 1974 amendments narrowed the types of documents that the government could withhold, imposed a timetable for complying with FOIA requests, and threatened officials with administrative sanctions for wrongfully withholding documents.

In 2019, members of the public and the press made 858,952 requests for information from the 118 federal agencies covered by FOIA. The media produced more than four thousand news stories using the documents they obtained.

Giving people the right to demand information did not solve the immediate problems of reforming the nation's intelligence agencies and restoring trust in the government. President Gerald Ford took the first step toward rebuilding confidence in the FBI and CIA in 1976 when he reaffirmed the ban on spying on domestic groups and prohibited the National Security Agency from intercepting communications inside the United States.

The Justice Department adopted strict guidelines prohibiting the FBI from investigating any individual or group based on activities protected by the First Amendment. It could launch a preliminary investigation only when there was evidence of an intent to break the law, and the case could not continue more than ninety days or involve the use of informants, wiretaps, or mail "covers" unless there were "specific and articulable facts" supporting the suspicion of illegal intent.

Congress also increased its oversight of the nation's intelligence agencies. In 1976, the Senate created the Select Committee on Intelligence; the House organized its own intelligence committee a couple of months later.

By the late 1970s, Vietnam, Watergate, and the intelligence scandals had helped create a movement for greater openness at all levels of government. State legislatures and local governments began opening their records to public access for the first time. Many also enacted open meeting laws that strictly limited the amount of public business that elected officials could transact behind closed doors.

Lawsuits often accomplished what public officials were unwilling to do voluntarily. People who had participated in protests during the 1960s sued police in New York, Chicago, Los Angeles, and Memphis for spying on them. Public officials signed agreements that barred illegal surveillance in the future.

Sometimes politicians even took the lead in controlling the police. In 1979, the Seattle City Council responded to the news that its police department had spied on 750 residents by passing an ordinance setting strict limits on the department's intelligence gathering and providing for an auditor to ensure compliance.

The 1960s and 1970s gave American citizens more freedom to express themselves than at any time in United States history, probably more than anyone had ever possessed. In the years ahead, many would argue that the country had gone too far.

THE FIGHT CONTINUES

Not everyone embraced the revolution.

In 1961, publisher Barney Rosset learned that the hard way. Having successfully published *Lady Chatterley's Lover*, he decided to push his luck. He convinced author Henry Miller to allow him to issue his novel *Tropic of Cancer*, a far more sexually explicit book that had become an underground classic since its publication in Paris in 1934.

At first, things went better than even Rosset could have hoped. The Justice Department declared that the book was not obscene under the new definition set forth in the Supreme Court's recent decision in the *Roth* case. Officials in the post office and the customs bureau fell in line. Rosset was ecstatic as orders poured in from around the country. Grove Press received so many orders that it had to print additional copies five times before the book's release. More than sixty-eight thousand copies sold in the first week.

Rosset was still taking a huge risk. State and local officials were not required to listen to the Justice Department. Almost all of the states and many cities had obscenity laws, and there was growing pressure on local authorities to enforce them.

In 1957, a Cincinnati attorney, Charles H. Keating Jr., had organized Citizens for Decent Literature (CDL) to clean up the town. CDL provided the police both political support and legal advice on how to prosecute obscenity cases, which were relatively rare. As CDL grew into a national organization with more than two hundred affiliated groups, obscenity arrests rose. But no one anticipated what was about to happen to booksellers, wholesalers, and magazine distributors who sold *Tropic of Cancer*.

Police officials throughout the country began by issuing "unofficial" warnings that the book was obscene. Such warnings were sufficient to suppress *Tropic of Cancer* in many places. Frightened wholesalers and retailers returned six hundred thousand books to Grove. Then the arrests started. Although 2.5 million copies were in print by the end of 1961, it was impossible to buy the book in most parts of the country.

Keating and his supporters hoped that the Supreme Court would uphold the prosecutions. However, in 1964, it reaffirmed its decision that material can be banned only if it is "utterly without redeeming social importance." The censors were outraged. "These decisions cannot be accepted quietly by the American people if the nation is to survive," a group of Catholic, Protestant, and Jewish religious leaders declared.[1]

The protest over obscenity reflected a deep dissatisfaction among many Americans over the nation's direction that would soon blossom into a great conservative wave. After decades out of power, conservatives finally nominated one of their own — Barry Goldwater — as the Republican candidate for president in 1964. They redoubled their efforts after Goldwater's defeat, exploiting the divisions created in American society by the civil rights, antiwar, and women's liberation movements.

Conservatives blamed changes in the media for a loosening of sexual mores. In 1968, the motion picture industry abandoned decades of self-censorship in favor of a rating system that allowed patrons to decide for themselves how much sex and violence they wanted to see.

Television and radio also began to relax the self-imposed guidelines that restricted content. The TV networks developed dramas, situation comedies, and soap operas that depicted characters who were divorced, unfaithful, even pregnant and unwed. At the same time, sexually explicit material increasingly entered the mainstream. Hugh Hefner had founded *Playboy* magazine in 1953, and by the 1960s men's magazines were available on newsstands and in drugstores in many parts of the country. "Adult" bookstores sold "hard-core" pornography depicting sex acts, and adult theaters proliferated in most large cities.

In 1967, members of Congress created the National Commission on Obscenity and Pornography to demonstrate the harmful effects of pornography. They were horrified when the commission concluded that there was no evidence to support restricting adult access to sexually explicit material and recommended legalizing it. Members of the Senate repudiated the commission's conclusions by a vote of 60–5.

President Richard Nixon also condemned the report and began to reshape the Supreme Court. He appointed four justices, giving conservatives control. In 1973, in the case of *Miller v. California*, the Nixon appointees joined in significantly expanding the definition of obscenity. No longer would it be necessary to prove material was "utterly without social value" for it to be legally banned, although material would still be exempt if it had "serious" value.

The court also declared that local communities could apply their own standards in defining obscenity, making it possible for a jury in a conservative city or town to send someone to prison for producing or distributing material that was not illegal elsewhere.

In 1980, the election of President Ronald Reagan gave a powerful boost to the conservative censorship campaign. The first evidence was a sudden jump in the number of challenges to books used in schools and libraries.

More than eight hundred challenges occurred every year in the early 1980s as conservative parents took aim at a wide range of material, including books by Judy Blume and other authors who were writing about sex and other problems that confronted adolescents. Conservatives also attacked books for "offensive" language and portraying "anti-family" values.

Meanwhile, anti-pornography activists pressured the Reagan

administration to take strong action against sexually explicit material. The result was the creation of the Attorney General Edwin Meese's Commission on Pornography, which was stacked with people who supported vigorous enforcement of the obscenity laws. Retailers received the message.

Without waiting for the commission's final report, the Southland Corporation, the owner of forty-five hundred 7-Eleven stores, stopped selling *Playboy* and *Penthouse* and recommended that thirty-six hundred franchise stores do the same. Other chains followed suit. Within months, seventeen thousand stores no longer carried the magazines.

The removal of *Playboy*, *Penthouse*, and other men's magazines from stores across the country had a domino effect, causing retailers in some parts of the country to drop other controversial material, including magazines about rock-and-roll music, several teen magazines, the swimsuit issue of *Sports Illustrated*, and issues of *American Photographer* and *Cosmopolitan*.

Activists also targeted recordings. In 1985, at the urging of the Parents Music Resource Center, a group created by Elizabeth "Tipper" Gore, the wife of Tennessee Democratic senator Al Gore, the Senate Commerce Committee held hearings on the increasingly graphic sexual and violent content in rap and other forms of popular music.

The music industry agreed to put warning labels on recordings that parents might object to their children buying, but some law enforcement officials were not satisfied. The sheriff of Broward County, Florida, warned retailers that they would face arrest for selling albums by the rap group 2 Live Crew, and an Alabama record store owner was prosecuted for selling a 2 Live Crew album. An appeals court overturned the storeowner's conviction, but prosecutors had sent a clear message that retailers exercised their First Amendment rights at their peril.

Not even museums were immune in the campaign against

Demonstrators express support for an exhibition by Robert Mapplethorpe

indecency. In 1990, Cincinnati authorities prosecuted museum director Dennis Barrie for obscenity and child pornography for exhibiting works by photographer Robert Mapplethorpe. Barrie was acquitted.

The efforts of local law enforcement paled beside the ambition of the Justice Department's new National Obscenity Enforcement Unit, which launched a campaign aimed at destroying the fourteen largest mail-order distributors of sexual material. Justice Department officials made it clear to the owners of these businesses that they would not permit them to distribute even constitutionally protected material like *Playboy* and *The Joy of Sex*.

In early 1989, conservative activists opened a new front in their fight against indecency, which the media had begun to describe as a "culture war." They learned that the National Endowment for the Arts had provided funding for an exhibit that included a photograph titled *Piss Christ*. The photograph by Andres Serrano depicted a crucifix submerged in a jar filled with the artist's urine.

Members of Congress expressed horror. They charged that the NEA was using tax money to support "pornographic, anti-Christian 'works of art,'" and quickly approved legislation that barred it from giving grants to artists whose work "might be deemed obscene."

Groups like the ACLU, Freedom to Read Foundation, Media Coalition, National Coalition Against Censorship, and People for the American Way worked hard to contain the threat posed by the anti-pornography movement. They testified against restrictive legislation, filed lawsuits to challenge statues they considered unconstitutional, and undertook a number of important public relations initiatives.

One of the most lasting efforts began in 1982 when librarians and booksellers celebrated the first Banned Books Week, which remains the only national event celebrating the freedom to read. The ACLU met the challenge of the Attorney General's Commission on Pornography — the Meese Commission — by assigning one of its smartest spokesmen to dog the heels of the commission as it traveled from city to city, pointing out its flaws to the local press.

The National Coalition Against Censorship held a national conference, "The Meese Commission Exposed," during which leading writers and artists warned against the dangers of censorship. After the attack on the NEA, both the ACLU and People for the American Way aggressively campaigned for the endangered agency. The ACLU created an Art Censorship Project to coordinate its efforts.

The American Booksellers Association (ABA) was particularly aggressive in beefing up its ability to respond to censorship threats. Throughout the 1980s, booksellers had strongly opposed the growing pressure for censorship. In 1986, they joined magazine wholesalers and distributors in founding Americans for Constitutional Freedom to oppose the recommendations of the Meese Commission.

In February 1989, censorship fears reached a new level when Iran's Ayatollah Ruhollah Khomeini issued a fatwa calling for the execution of Salman Rushdie, the author of *Satanic Verses*, a novel that many Muslims considered blasphemous. Arsonists bombed a number of bookstores around the world, including two in Berkeley, California.

The ABA responded to the crisis by establishing the American Booksellers Foundation for Free Expression. Arts organizations created the National Campaign for Freedom of Expression to oppose content restrictions on NEA grants.

The anti-censorship groups depended heavily on volunteers. Throughout the 1980s, publishers, librarians, booksellers, record and video store owners, writers, artists, and concerned citizens spoke out against censorship. They fought challenges to books in their local library, mounted displays during Banned Books Week, and joined in filing briefs to support plaintiffs in important legal cases.

Women dressed as Keystone Kops wearing buttons identifying them as the SEX POLICE picketed a public hearing by the Meese Commission. However, feminists did not all agree on the pornography issue. Many supported Catharine A. MacKinnon, a law professor who had come to believe that pornography was the major obstacle in women's search for equality.

MacKinnon had immersed herself in radical politics at Yale University during the early 1970s, fighting racial injustice with the Black Panther Party, protesting the Vietnam War, and joining the new women's movement. The women's movement was such a powerful influence that MacKinnon postponed work on her PhD in political science to enter Yale Law School, where she resolved to do something about the fact that the law had "nothing whatever to do with the problem of sexual inequality as it's experienced by women."[2]

On graduating from law school, MacKinnon started teaching Yale's first women's studies course. She knew very well that

Comstock and his supporters had prosecuted feminist heroes like Emma Goldman, Margaret Sanger, and Mary Ware Dennett. However, she became convinced that censorship was necessary to protect women.

Feminists suffered a number of serious defeats in the late 1970s. Only four years after establishing a constitutional right to abortion, the Supreme Court limited the effect of its ruling by declaring that the government could not be compelled to pay for the abortions of poor women. The fight for the Equal Rights Amendment was foundering. To many, it seemed that the women's movement itself was on the verge of collapse.

During this period of disillusion, MacKinnon and other feminists began to insist that violence against women was a bigger obstacle to sexual equality than child-rearing practices or job discrimination. They believed that sexually explicit material reinforced sexist attitudes, and a growing number became convinced that it also incited rape.

MacKinnon recognized that the Supreme Court had made it impossible to suppress sexually explicit material unless it met the legal definition of obscenity, which required that it lack "serious" literary, artistic, political, or scientific value. However, she believed that if she could prove pornography was not speech at all but a form of sex discrimination, then it could be banned as a violation of the civil rights of women.

The Indianapolis City Council passed an ordinance that adopted her definition of pornography in 1984. Fearing that it would result in the suppression of First Amendment–protected material, publishers, booksellers, librarians, and magazine distributors immediately challenged the ordinance in court.

US District Court judge Sarah Evans Barker declared the law unconstitutional, rejecting MacKinnon's claim that sexually explicit material is not speech. She also reminded MacKinnon and her supporters that "in terms of altering sociological patterns, much as alteration may be necessary and desirable, free speech, rather than being the enemy, is a long-tested and worthy ally."[3]

The division among feminists reemerged in 1991 over the Pornography Victims' Compensation Act, a bill introduced in the US Senate that authorized the victim of a sex crime to sue the producer and distributor of material that is both "sexually explicit" and "violent" if the material was "a proximate cause" of the crime. The provisions of the federal bill were breathtaking. It targeted speech protected by the First Amendment, making producers and distributors of legal works liable for the crimes committed by others. Random House, which had just published Brett Easton Ellis's controversial novel *American Psycho*, could be sued by the victim of an assault inspired by the book, as could the retailer who sold it to the attacker. One provision of the bill allowed the criminal himself to testify on how the pornographic material had caused his crime.

Media groups responded strongly. Eighteen trade associations presented a legal memo to the Senate Judiciary Committee demonstrating that third-party liability was a drastic departure from legal tradition that would weaken the ability of the courts to hold criminals responsible for their crimes.

A revised bill applied only to legally obscene material, but publishers, booksellers, librarians, magazine wholesalers and distributors, and video retailers remained strongly opposed to the legislation because of the chilling effect that it would have on the sale of material with sexual content that was not obscene.

Several key members of the committee agreed with them, including Joseph Biden of Delaware, a Democrat, and Hank Brown, a Republican from Colorado. Biden and Brown raised questions during committee hearings that defeated hopes for a quick victory and gave critics of the bill a chance to organize.

They received support from Americans for Constitutional Freedom, which released a report demonstrating that there was no credible scientific evidence that sexually explicit material causes violence against women.

The same argument appeared in a *New York Times* op-ed written by Teller, a comedian who burlesqued the notion that "if we stop showing rape in movies people will stop committing it in real life": "Give us a break! When one pays $7 to go into a theater to see big pictures moving on a wall, one does not have to be a mental giant to realize you are watching a movie. It makes you wonder how they explain the millions of people who saw 'Psycho' without stealing bankrolls or bumping off blondes." When people started laughing at the Pornography Victims' Compensation Act, its opponents knew they had a chance to kill it.[4]

Feminists delivered the death blow. Anti-censorship feminists protested that the issue of pornography was distracting women from the fight against the real sources of sexual inequality in American society and warned against the danger of making a political alliance with conservatives who opposed the major goals of the women's movement.

The fight against the Pornography Victims' Compensation Act revealed that a solid majority of American feminists remained strongly opposed to censorship. While the national board of the National Organization for Women did not take a position on the bill, five state chapters, including New York and California, announced their opposition.

The Ad Hoc Committee of Feminists for Free Expression opposed the bill (S. 1521) in a letter to the Judiciary Committee signed by 180 prominent women, including Betty Friedan, Adrienne Rich, Judy Blume, Nora Ephron, Erica Jong, Susan Isaacs, and Jamaica Kincaid. "[S. 1521] scapegoats speech as a substitute for action against violence," the letter said. "Rape, battery and child molestation are vicious crimes that this nation should take every measure to eliminate. But S. 1521 will do crime victims more harm than good."[5] The Judiciary Committee finally approved the Pornography Victims' Compensation Act, but it never advanced further.

After nearly two decades of struggle, the anti-pornography movement was beginning to weaken, but it still possessed one powerful issue — child protection. In 1996, the movement used the strong popular support for keeping kids safe to pass the Communications Decency Act (CDA), the first effort by Congress to censor the burgeoning internet.

The nation's lawmakers had little understanding of the complexities of this new electronic medium, but they had heard that it exposed children to sexually explicit material, and that was all they needed to know. Without holding any hearings, they banned the posting of any "indecent" or "patently offensive" material anywhere that minors could see it. The Supreme Court made short work of the CDA, ruling in a near-unanimous decision in 1997 that the law was unconstitutional because it forced the removal of material that adults had a First Amendment right to see.

The culture war was over. A real war was about to begin.

Homeland Security

In the week after the attacks on September 11, 2001, Americans were afraid and angry. They watched the collapse of the World Trade Center endlessly rebroadcast on television. Residents of New York and Washington heard the sounds of fighter jets patrolling overhead. In the subways, soldiers stood guard with automatic weapons. US bombers hit al-Qaeda terrorist camps in Afghanistan just three weeks later, hoping to kill Osama bin Laden. American ground troops followed in a campaign that swiftly ousted the Afghani Taliban leaders who had protected him.

Civil libertarians were also alarmed. Three days after the 9/11 attacks, representatives of dozens of civil rights and civil liberties groups jammed the conference room on the ground floor of the

ACLU office in Washington. The crowd spilled outside into an adjoining garden; others listened from the hallway, sitting on the staircase that led to the offices above.

Morton Halperin, a former ACLU official, expressed what was in the minds of many of his colleagues in an email on the day after the attacks. "There can be no doubt that we will hear calls in the next few days for Congress to enact sweeping legislation to deal with terrorism," he wrote. "This will include not only the secrecy provision, but also broad authority to conduct electronic and other surveillance and to investigate political groups."[6]

During the meeting at the ACLU, a new group, In Defense of Freedom Coalition, was organized, and work began on a ten-point statement that was released the following week with the support of more than 150 religious, civil rights, and civil liberties groups. Three hundred law professors also signed the statement.

The danger soon became apparent. Police arrested more than a thousand Muslim men from Arab and other foreign countries and held them incommunicado without any evidence that they were involved in terrorism. In jail, guards assaulted some of the "terrorists."

Private media outlets punished employees for criticizing the government. Comedian Bill Maher outraged Americans when he said on his television show that piloting airliners into the World Trade Center was braver than firing missiles into Afghanistan. Although he apologized, the ABC television network did not renew his contract. Two weekly newspapers fired editors for columns and editorials accusing President George W. Bush of cowardice because he did not immediately return to Washington after the attacks.

The atmosphere for free speech was ugly on college campuses as well. On the morning of the 9/11 attacks, a history professor at the University of New Mexico jokingly told his class: "Anyone who can blow up the Pentagon gets my vote." He was promptly suspended.

Conservative critics thought the problem went considerably deeper than bad jokes. The American Council of Trustees and Alumni denounced professors as "the weak link in America's response to terrorism" because they were pointing "accusatory fingers, not at the terrorists, but at America itself." They published a report that listed 117 allegedly anti-American statements made on college campuses.[7]

A new group, Americans for Victory Over Terrorism, expanded the list of people "who are attempting to use this opportunity to promulgate their agenda of 'blame American first'" to include legislators, authors, and columnists.[8]

Even more alarming to civil libertarians was the introduction of a 350-page bill that was to become the centerpiece of the government's fight against terrorism — the USA Patriot Act.

The Patriot Act increased the power of the government to engage in secret searches. Its most chilling provision made it possible for the FBI to seize vast amounts of personal data about American citizens in the dragnet that it was deploying for terrorists. Section 215 authorized the FBI to seek warrants to seize "any tangible things" that it needed "for an authorized investigation . . . to protect against international terrorism or clandestine intelligence activities." It applied to all organizations, including nonprofits and charities.[9]

While government had long enjoyed the right to issue subpoenas, it normally had to show that there was "probable cause" to believe that a crime had been committed. Under Section 215, however, the government was required to show only that the records were "sought for" a terrorism or espionage investigation.

Finally, the whole process of securing the records was cloaked in secrecy. The FBI would request the order from a secret court established by the Foreign Intelligence Surveillance Act (FISA), and the order would contain a gag provision that prevented the recipient from revealing its existence to anyone other than a person whose

President George W. Bush signs the USA Patriot Act in the East Room of the White House, 2001

assistance was necessary to provide the documents. It was not even clear whether the recipient could consult a lawyer. But even if a lawyer was called, there seemed no other option than to comply. Section 215 made no provision for challenging the order in court.

There were expressions of concern about the Patriot Act in both the House and the Senate, but Attorney General John Ashcroft rejected all efforts to amend the bill. Congress overwhelmingly approved it just six weeks after 9/11.

Amid rising fear over threats to civil liberties, a grassroots movement stirred in isolated spots around the country. Activists in Northampton, Massachusetts, formed a Bill of Rights Defense Committee. It urged the city council to approve a resolution committing "local law enforcement [to] continue to preserve residents' freedom of speech, religion, assembly and privacy . . . even if requested or authorized to infringe upon these rights by federal law enforcement acting under new powers granted by the USA Patriot Act."[10]

By the time Northampton approved the resolution in May 2002, the city councils in Ann Arbor, Michigan, Denver, Colorado, and

Amherst and Leverett, Massachusetts, had passed similar legislation. Four more approved resolutions in the next eight weeks, including Cambridge, Massachusetts, and Boulder, Colorado.

While the origins of the movement clearly lay in college towns with large liberal constituencies, the Bill of Rights Defense Committee believed that its message had broad appeal and began to offer information and advice to activists in communities throughout the country. The ACLU quickly realized the movement's potential. It announced that it would encourage the movement to pass local and state legislation "prohibiting local law enforcement participation in repressive Administration initiatives." It also began running a thirty-second television commercial that urged people to "Look what John Ashcroft is doing to our Constitution."[11]

The civil libertarians faced an uphill struggle. The fear of a new attack was strong, and public opinion polls showed overwhelming support for the administration's policies.

The Patriot Act, however, gave civil libertarians a tangible target to aim for. It contained two sections that members of the public might find truly alarming: Section 213 allowed the government to conduct secret searches in any criminal investigation, delaying notification for a "reasonable" period. The so-called sneak and peak warrants generated a great deal of controversy, prompting the House of Representatives to try cutting off federal funding for such searches. But it was Section 215 that captured the nation's imagination. In part, this was because it deeply worried two large groups — the nation's librarians and booksellers.

The librarians had already had a bad experience with the FBI. In 1987, they learned that its agents had been secretly requesting the borrowing records of suspected Soviet agents. They were alarmed that the government was attempting to turn them into informers and had apparently succeeded in obtaining information from some of their colleagues. To restore confidence in the confidentiality of library records, state library associations launched a highly successful campaign to pass state privacy laws banning the release of library records except in compliance with a court order.

The moment of truth for booksellers had occurred a decade later when Kenneth Starr, a special prosecutor investigating potential crimes by President Bill Clinton, subpoenaed two Washington bookstores in an effort to identify books purchased by Monica Lewinsky, a White House intern who was suspected of having a sexual relationship with Clinton.

The subpoena surprised booksellers. Unaware that computer inventory systems were a potential source of information about their customers, they sued to block the Starr subpoena, arguing that government demands for reading records would have a chilling effect on free speech. A judge agreed, narrowing Starr's subpoena to include only records directly relevant to his case.

Librarians and booksellers were stunned when they learned that the federal government could use Section 215 to force them to turn over patron records. They were afraid that people would not feel free to buy or borrow the books they wanted if they knew the government was reading over their shoulder.

The first sign of resistance appeared in the fall of 2002 when the Vermont Library Association sent an open letter to the state's congressional delegation, urging the repeal of the provisions of Section 215 that threatened reader privacy. Bernie Sanders, Vermont's sole representative in the House, held a press conference and, with a bookseller and a librarian at his side, announced that he would lead the fight to amend Section 215. "This is a crashing, crushing attack on basic rights in this country, and it's got to be opposed," Sanders said.[12]

Sanders introduced the Freedom to Read Protection Act in early 2003 that exempted bookstore and library records from Section 215. It became a rallying point for those worried about the threats to civil liberties and received strong editorial support from major newspapers. Its 118 cosponsors included 13 Republicans.[13]

Other signs of dissent included a dramatic increase in the number of cities and towns passing anti–Patriot Act resolutions. In 2002 and 2003, forty-one communities approved resolutions.

Attorney General Ashcroft struck back against the critics of Section 215. "The law enforcement community has no interest in your reading habits," he declared. "The hysteria is ridiculous." The movement continued to grow. The American Library Association, the American Booksellers Association, and PEN American Center, an authors' group, launched the Campaign for Reader Privacy to rally support for the Freedom to Read Protection Act. It started a petition campaign in bookstores and libraries that collected more than 120,000 signatures in its first three months.[14]

Activists were also fighting for civil liberties in the courts. Although many different civil rights, press, and advocacy groups sued the government, the ACLU and its state affiliates once again played a predominant role in the struggle. In the five years after 9/11, they filed more than eighty lawsuits.

Most of the First Amendment cases grew out of the clash between authorities and people protesting the use of American troops in Afghanistan and Iraq. So-called free speech zones that authorities created to keep anti-war protesters far removed from the site of speeches by the president and other members of the administration were just one example of repressive measures.

One of the free speech cases involved Bretton Barber, a high school junior in Dearborn Heights, Michigan. School officials sent Barber home from school for wearing a T-shirt with a picture of President Bush and the words INTERNATIONAL TERRORIST. Barber knew his rights. He was well aware of the US Supreme Court decision in *Tinker v. Des Moines Independent School District*, the case that upheld the right of students to wear armbands protesting the Vietnam War. A federal judge upheld his right to protest.

Many of the other cases failed. Yet, slowly, the courts began to assert themselves. While the ACLU had little luck in challenging free speech zones, it succeeded in many of the cases that it brought over local efforts to restrict protests.

In the spring of 2005, Congress became the center of the fight over the Patriot Act. The sponsors of the law had agreed at the time of its passage that some of its most controversial provisions, including Section 215, would expire in four years unless Congress reauthorized them. It was widely assumed that Congress would approve an extension without any changes that would address the concerns of civil libertarians.

The first indication of the fight ahead came when Bernie Sanders attempted to pass the Freedom to Read Act by adding it as an amendment to a House appropriations bill. He had tried the same thing the year before and had come within a few votes of success. This time the amendment was adopted with the near-unanimous support of Democrats and thirty-eight Republicans.

Six weeks later, the Senate unanimously approved a Patriot Act reauthorization bill that included important safeguards for civil liberties, including a provision that narrowed the FBI's authority to seek records under Section 215. However, the Senate bill had to be reconciled with legislation passed by the House. When the conference committee met, it eliminated many of the important reforms in the Senate bill.

Civil libertarians were understandably disappointed, but the final bill did include a number of significant changes. It explicitly recognized that people who receive Section 215 orders and National Security Letters, another secret demand for information, have the right to consult an attorney and to challenge them in court. It also required the director of the FBI to personally authorize all bookstore and library searches under Section 215.

The reauthorization bill also expanded congressional oversight of the operation of the Patriot Act by requiring the Justice Department to provide annual reports of the number of Section

215s ordered and National Security Letters it issued, including how many were sent to bookstores and libraries.

Taken together, the Patriot Act reforms approved by Congress began the process of establishing accountability for the government's secret powers. Equally important, the fight to amend the Patriot Act reform movement made civil liberties a central issue in the debate over the war on terrorism. This was a significant achievement. The fear of new attacks was still strong, and the president's party controlled both houses of Congress.

Civil libertarians had achieved successes by reaching out directly to the American people. The ACLU's membership had grown to four hundred thousand, a 40 percent increase since 9/11. The Bill of Rights Defense Committee's campaign passed resolutions in four hundred communities and eight state legislatures. The Campaign for Reader Privacy mobilized more than a hundred thousand bookstore customers and library patrons.

The fight to limit the government's secret surveillance continued in ensuing years. It received a dramatic boost in 2013 when Edward Snowden, a CIA employee, revealed that the government was using Section 215 to conduct a mass surveillance program that included collecting the phone records of all American citizens.

Free Speech Becomes Controversial

During the first decades of the twenty-first century, the political divisions over free speech became increasingly complex. They had never been entirely clear-cut. While liberals had generally led the fight against censorship, conservatives who identified themselves as libertarians shared a desire to keep government out of the private lives of American citizens. Libertarians had played an important role in preventing the Patriot Act from being any more intrusive and potent than it was by insisting on "sunsets" for Section 215 and other controversial provisions.

On the other hand, many liberals had supported the suppression of Communists during the Cold War. They split again during the culture wars of the 1980s, a decade of disillusion for many who hoped to see the triumph of the so-called rights revolution that began in the 1950s. Catharine MacKinnon was not the only progressive who saw the First Amendment as an obstacle to reform.

Race relations were deteriorating as the number of Black, Hispanic, and Asian American students on college campuses increased. In 1986 and 1987, there was an outburst of racism, including many incidents at the nation's elite institutions.

In January 1987, Black students at the University of Michigan discovered handbills in their dormitory lounge declaring "open season" on "saucer lips, porch monkeys and jigaboos." A few days later, a disc jockey on the campus radio station invited listeners to tell racist jokes on the air.[15]

Tensions increased when students who had gathered to protest these incidents saw someone display a Ku Klux Klan uniform in a dormitory window. A second handbill was found that said Blacks should be "hanging from the trees," not attending college.

The university responded by creating a student code of conduct, the Policy on Discrimination and Discriminatory Harassment of Students, that prohibited "any behavior, verbal or physical, that stigmatizes or victimizes an individual on the basis of race, ethnicity, religion, sex, sexual orientation, creed, national origin, ancestry, age, marital status, handicap or Vietnam-era veteran status."[16]

The broad ban on speech alarmed civil libertarians. It applied to all offensive remarks, not just insults addressed to individuals. It also failed to exempt speech that occurred in a classroom, posing a serious threat to academic freedom. The university inadvertently confirmed the danger of censorship by releasing a student guide to the policy that gave as an example of prohibited conduct a male student commenting in class that "women students just aren't as good in this field as men."[17]

A psychology student who feared that any discussion of racial and gender differences would become impossible challenged the policy in court. A judge struck it down as a violation of the First Amendment, citing three cases in which the university punished or threatened to punish students for things they said in class.

Despite the failure of the Michigan policy, support within the academic community for speech codes was growing. Several legal scholars observed that the First Amendment was not absolute. The Supreme Court had upheld restrictions on speech that is libelous or promotes criminal acts, including bribery, fraud, and criminal conspiracy. It had supported the banning of direct threats, harassment, and incitement to violence.

Like MacKinnon, these scholars insisted that the Fourteenth Amendment, which promised equal protection of the laws to all citizens, was just as important as the First Amendment. They argued that this meant taking steps to ensure a non-hostile campus environment.

University administrators rushed to adopt speech codes, believing that they were necessary to maintain peace. By 1990, 60 percent of universities and colleges were operating under new rules for student conduct, although none were as restrictive as the one struck down in Michigan.

However, the legal status of the new speech restrictions came into question following a Supreme Court decision in 1992. The court ruled on the constitutionality of a St. Paul, Minnesota, ordinance that was passed in response to a cross burning on the lawn of a Black family. The ordinance banned the display of any object that "arouses anger, alarm or resentment in others on the basis of race, color, creed, religion or gender."

The justices were unanimous in striking down the law as a prohibition of protected speech. They also pointed out that the municipality had other laws that made it possible to punish the cross burning without infringing on free speech.[18]

By reaffirming previous cases that upheld the right to engage in hate speech, it appeared that the Supreme Court might overturn speech codes. Some public universities and colleges, which are government institutions and subject to the First Amendment, dropped or amended their policies.

Twenty years later, during another period of racial unrest, the controversy over free speech on campus reemerged. In 2013, a new civil rights group, Black Lives Matter, began to demand an end to police violence against Black people. The next year, rioting erupted in Ferguson, Missouri, a suburb of St. Louis, after a police officer shot and killed Michael Brown, a young Black man.

In November 2015, the protests over racial discrimination spread to campuses across the country. At the University of Missouri, there were demonstrations over the failure of the administration to respond to racist incidents. The president and other university officials resigned. At Yale, a controversy erupted over the wearing of racially insensitive Halloween costumes.

Some of the protests advocated actions threatening to free speech. During a demonstration at Missouri, a faculty member urged protesters to use "muscle" to stop a student journalist from taking pictures. Students at Wesleyan University attempted to defund the student newspaper because it published an opinion piece that raised questions about Black Lives Matter. At Amherst, students demanded that school officials punish the creators of a poster lamenting the decline of free speech on campus.

Activists proposed new measures to protect people of color from hate speech. They asserted that even expressions that are not overtly racist are harmful. While these microaggressions occur throughout society, they urged special care in classrooms and urged professors to provide trigger warnings prior to the introduction of content that might be upsetting to some people. They also advocated for the creation of safe spaces where students could gather without fear of being offended.

In February 2017, students at the University of California at Berkeley went even further. With the support of a hundred faculty members, they demanded that the university cancel an appearance by Milo Yiannopoulos, a right-wing firebrand.

Administrators refused. Berkeley was proud of its history as the home of the free speech movement. However, university officials changed their minds when a small group broke off from a peaceful protest rally and began throwing firecrackers, setting fires, and smashing windows. They canceled the speech.

Later that summer, white supremacists held a protest in Charlottesville, the home of the University of Virginia. In a frightening echo of Nazi rallies, hundreds of chanting white men marched with torches through the streets of the small city. The next day they rioted, exchanging blows with counter-protesters.

The Unite the Right rally shocked the nation. Outrage grew after President Donald Trump refused to condemn it, even after a white supremacist hit a counter-protester with his car, killing her. Trump insisted there were "very fine people on both sides." Fear over the possibility of further disturbances led several public universities to bar speaking events by Richard Spencer, a prominent neo-Nazi and featured speaker at Unite the Right.

Avowed racists were not the only ones meeting opposition on college campuses. In 2017, two hundred students at Middlebury College disrupted an appearance by Charles Murray, a political scientist, because they considered his controversial book *The Bell Curve* to be racist. When Murray rose to speak, students turned their backs. After reading a statement, they began chanting, "Hey, hey, ho, ho, Charles Murray has got to go."

Organizers had invited a left-leaning professor to lead a conversation with Murray after his prepared remarks. They had also set aside time for members of the audience to question him. However, the chanting made it impossible for Murray to speak and the event was canceled. A number of students accosted Murray and the professor as they attempted to leave, injuring the faculty member. The college later disciplined sixty-seven students for their role in the protest.[19]

De-platforming attempts became frequent at colleges and universities. In the same year as the Middlebury incident, there were forty-four "disinvitation" events, according to the Foundation for Individual Rights in Education (FIRE). More than half succeeded in canceling a speech.

It wasn't just college kids who were growing impatient with free speech. Over the previous decade, many liberals had been dismayed when conservative justices on the Supreme Court cited the First Amendment as justification for striking down regulations approved by Democratic administrations.

The most notorious decision came in 2010 in *Citizens United v. Federal Election Commission*, a challenge to the Bipartisan Campaign Reform Act (BCRA). The law banned "independent" expenditures by corporations and unions in political campaigns. Direct contributions to political parties and candidates were already illegal.

Citizens United, a conservative advocacy group, challenged the law when the Federal Election Commission ruled that a film it had produced, *Hillary: The Movie*, could not be aired shortly before the 2008 Democratic primaries because it was an "electioneering communication" specifically prohibited by BCRA.

In a 5–4 decision that split the justices along ideological lines, the court declared that the ban on independent expenditures was unconstitutional. Writing for the majority, Justice Anthony Kennedy said the First Amendment bars the government from deciding who can speak. "If the First Amendment has any force, it prohibits Congress from fining or jailing citizens, for simply engaging in political speech."[20]

Kennedy observed that the ban was potentially far-reaching, applying to all corporations, including nonprofits involved in advocacy. The ACLU underscored this point in a brief urging the court to overturn BCRA. It noted that in the months before the 1972 election, *The New York Times*, citing an earlier campaign finance law, had initially refused to publish an ACLU ad that criticized President Richard Nixon.

Justice John Paul Stevens responded with an impassioned, ninety-page dissent, parts of which he read in court on the day the decision was announced. He argued that the majority was making a terrible mistake by giving corporations the same free speech rights as citizens. Business corporations are far more powerful because they have the money to bend politicians to their will. The appearance of corruption will undermine faith in America's political institutions and discourage participation in the political process, he said.

"At bottom, the Court's opinion is thus a rejection of the common sense of the American people, who have recognized a need to prevent corporations from undermining self-government since the days of Theodore Roosevelt," Stevens concluded.[21]

Liberals joined Stevens in his fury. President Barack Obama denounced the decision during his State of the Union address a few days later. With the members of the Supreme Court sitting in front of him in the House of Representatives, Obama accused the majority of reversing "a century of law to open the floodgates of special interests — including foreign corporations — to spend without limit in our elections."[22]

Eight years later, in June 2018, Supreme Court Justice Elena Kagan issued a blistering dissent in a case that crystallized the disillusionment that many liberals felt about the First Amendment.

In another 5–4 decision, the court had struck down an Illinois law that permitted unions to collect a fee from non-union members to pay for collective bargaining that benefited everyone covered by a contract. The majority argued that the law, which was similar to laws in twenty-two other states, violated the First Amendment rights of the non-union workers by forcing them to support a union message.

As the solicitor general in the Obama administration, Kagan had argued before the court in support of BCRA. In responding to this new defeat, she blasted the conservative justices, accusing them of "weaponizing" the First Amendment "by turning [it] into a sword and using it against workaday economic and regulatory policy."[23]

A few months later, support for free speech appeared to reach a new low. *The New Yorker*, a paragon of liberal thought, announced that during the upcoming New Yorker Festival, its editor, David Remnick, would interview Stephen K. Bannon, a founder of the far-right website *Breitbart News* and a close adviser to President Trump.

Many liberals were outraged, and when several celebrities withdrew from the festival in protest, Remnick canceled his planned interview of Bannon.

Censorship pressure had also been rising in the arts. Artists who are people of color protested a lack of representation at every level of the creative process, and they also accused white artists of engaging in cultural appropriation when they used elements of the arts that originated in their communities.

In 2017, there was a protest at the Whitney Museum of American Art over a painting by white artist Dana Schutz, who used as her subject the searing photograph of the mutilated body of Emmett Till, the Black teenager who became a civil rights martyr after he was murdered in Mississippi in 1955. "[I]t is not acceptable for a white person to transmute Black suffering into profit and fun," Hannah Black, a writer and artist, said. Whitney officials rejected her demand that they destroy the painting.[24]

Soon after, the Walker Art Center in Minnesota dismantled another artwork that had been criticized as a product of cultural appropriation. Artist Sam Durant had created a sculpture of a nineteenth-century scaffold outside the museum to draw attention to the cruelty of capital punishment. However, members of the Dakota tribe complained that the sculpture resembled the scaffold used to hang thirty-eight members of their tribe in 1862.

Critics of cultural appropriation also targeted literature. In 2018, *The Nation*, one of the country's leading opinion magazines, published a poem, "How-To," in which a street hustler offers advice on how to panhandle. The use of dialect suggested the hustler was Black, but the poet, Anderson Carlson-Wee, is white. When the editors began to hear complaints, they apologized for "the pain we have caused to the many communities affected by this poem."[25]

Pressure to censor was growing in book publishing as well. A movement emerged to encourage the publication of more books by people of color, and in some cases support for more diversity became demands for suppression. In 2016, critics took aim at *A Fine Dessert*, a picture book for young children that depicted how four families ate the same dessert during different periods of American history, including a mother and daughter who were enslaved on a southern plantation.

Reviewers loved the book, but others thought it was insufficiently critical of slavery. They objected strongly to an image of a young enslaved girl smiling. A similar criticism caused Scholastic, the largest publisher of children's books, to take the highly unusual step of withdrawing a book, *A Birthday Cake for George Washington*, which featured the president's enslaved cook.

Some of the protests came from within the publishing houses. Staff members questioned whether their employers should be releasing books by conservative authors or men accused of sexual abuse. When the Hachette Book Group announced plans to publish an autobiography by Woody Allen, whose daughter Dylan had accused him of sexually abusing her when she was seven, dozens of its employees staged a walkout, causing the cancellation of the book.

Several months later, during the first weeks of the protest over the murder of George Floyd, five publishing employees urged other staff members not to work during a "Day of Action" to show their support for Black Lives Matter and to demand greater diversity in the industry.

"We are disrupting and taking action by refusing to participate in a system complicit with white supremacy and racial capitalism for a day," they explained in a statement signed by thirteen hundred people. Their aims went beyond increasing diversity within the industry. One of their goals was to "pressure publishers to stop publishing racist books."[26]

By July 2020, liberals who sympathized with the goals of the new protest movement were beginning to express concern about the impact of de-platforming and other expressions of intolerance on the publishing industry and American culture generally.

A letter published in *Harper's Magazine* with the signatures of 153 prominent writers, journalists, and academics declared, "The free exchange of information and ideas, the lifeblood of a liberal society, is daily becoming more constricted." It condemned "an intolerance of opposing views, a vogue for public shaming and ostracism, and the tendency to dissolve complex policy issues in blinding moral certainty."[27]

Several writers responded promptly by circulating a letter endorsed by 150 people working in journalism and the arts, including many people of color. They rejected the idea that there was any serious threat to free speech. "The intellectual freedom of cis white intellectuals has never been under threat en masse," the letter said. "In fact they have never faced serious consequences — only momentary discomfort."[28]

Emotions were coming to a boil as the country approached the 2020 elections. Even before the voting began, Trump was claiming that only massive voter fraud could deny him a second term. When Biden won, Trump refused to accept the result by insisting without evidence that the election had been "stolen."

On January 6, 2021, at a rally in Washington, Trump urged his supporters to march to the Capitol to express their outrage. Hundreds of them surged up the steps and into the building, chasing members of Congress from the House chamber, where the official electoral vote was under way.

In the aftermath of the violence, the debate over free speech intensified. Citing the danger of further provocations by Trump, Facebook and Twitter banned him from their platforms. Google and Amazon accused Parler, a social media website popular with conservatives, of failing to enforce rules against hate speech. They withdrew their services, forcing it temporarily off the internet.

Simon & Schuster announced that it was withdrawing from its contract to publish a book by Senator Josh Hawley of Missouri, a Trump supporter, because of "his role in what became a dangerous threat to our democracy and freedom." The company also refused to distribute a book published by one of its client publishers that was written by one of the police officers in Louisville, Kentucky, who killed a young Black woman, Breonna Taylor, during a botched raid on her home.[29]

Several months later, more than two hundred Simon & Schuster employees signed a petition that asked the company to cancel its contract for a book by Vice President Mike Pence and pledge not to buy any books from members of the Trump administration. The company refused.

In April 2021, the publishing house W. W. Norton withdrew a biography of writer Philip Roth following accusations of sexual assault against its author, Blake Bailey.

Critics complained that attacks by progressives were creating a "cancel culture." At the same time, it was becoming clear once again that no one needed free speech protections more than the people who were demanding change.

Free Speech — The Indispensable Change Agent

From the beginning of our nation, free speech has been the indispensable tool in the struggle for change. It remains critically important to those who are fighting to realize important reforms, whether the issue is racial justice, sexual equality, gun violence, or climate change.

In the second decade of the twenty-first century, Americans witnessed the greatest era of protest since the civil rights and anti-war movements of the 1950s and 1960s. Like those activists — and the abolitionists, the suffragists, and the Wobblies before them — protesters confronted sometimes violent attacks on their right to free speech.

It is somewhat arbitrary to date the beginning of this new period of unrest. Activists organized Black Lives Matter in 2013. Protests erupted following the police shooting of Michael Brown in Ferguson, Missouri, in 2014.

National Football League player Colin Kaepernick's decision to stop standing during the "Star Spangled Banner" captured the nation's attention in 2016.

At first, Kaepernick, a quarterback for the San Francisco 49ers, simply remained seated on the bench. Then he began to kneel conspicuously on the sideline in an effort to protest racial inequality and the oppression of Black people in America. Another member of the team joined him, and soon NFL players around the league were participating in a national demonstration.

Kaepernick's act of conscience would ultimately cost him his athletic career. No NFL team offered him a contract after he left the 49ers.

But his example inspired others. Football players and other students in high schools and colleges across the country joined in kneeling or refusing to stand during the national anthem and the Pledge of Allegiance. School officials were outraged, and students

Women's March, 2017

were suspended. A teacher in Chicago attempted to drag a Black student to his feet during the pledge.

The country was in the midst of an election campaign and feelings were running high. Trump, a political novice, was using racist appeals to further his long-shot candidacy. He eagerly joined the controversy over the kneeling NFL players, who were predominantly Black. "They should try another country, see if they like it better," he said.[30]

By the time of the election, Trump had also alienated millions of women through his openly disrespectful and bullying treatment of his opponent, Hillary Clinton, and by promising to appoint Supreme Court justices who would repeal the right to an abortion. During the campaign, a tape surfaced revealing that Trump had said that he liked to force himself on women and "grab 'em by the pussy."[31]

Millions of women responded on the day after Trump's inauguration. Nearly half a million marched in Washington alone, more than at any time since the civil rights and anti-war marches in the 1960s. There were simultaneous marches in many major cities and smaller demonstrations in hundreds of towns. Between three and five million people participated.

Organizers of the march said its purpose was to send a message to the new administration that "women's rights are human rights." But they also announced their intention to fight for immigration reform, health care reform, disability justice, reproductive rights, the environment, LGBTQ rights, racial equality, freedom of religion, workers' rights, and tolerance.

In October 2017, one of the most important issues of the women's movement — sexual violence — became front-page news when *The New York Times* and *The New Yorker* reported that Harvey Weinstein, a prominent movie producer, had been accused by more than a dozen women of sexual harassment, assault, and rape.

Soon women began posting on social media the details of sexual abuse they had encountered in the workplace. In the following months, the #MeToo movement forced the resignations of dozens of prominent men in the media, finance, politics, and religion.

Controversy also grew over the treatment of Muslims, both in the United States and in Israel and its occupied territories. Trump had begun his presidency by issuing a ban on Muslims entering the United States from several Arab nations, purportedly to protect against another terrorist attack.

Many college students expressed support for Palestinians by joining a movement to Boycott, Divest and Sanction (BDS) Israel for its policies in the West Bank and Gaza. Israel and its supporters denounced BDS as anti-Semitic and launched a campaign that led thirty states to pass laws that prohibited companies from participating in the boycott. The ACLU and others have filed legal challenges to BDS laws because they punish speech that is critical of Israel. Several courts have agreed that BDS laws violate the First Amendment.

Free speech also became an issue in several well-publicized conflicts over environmental issues. In North Dakota, South

Dakota, and Louisiana, protesters attempted to halt the construction of oil pipelines that threatened Indigenous lands with pollution and would contribute to climate change. Thousands of Sioux Indians and their supporters established camps along the path of the Dakota Access Pipeline in North Dakota. Demonstrators clashed with police, who used pepper spray, tear gas, rubber bullets, and Tasers to respond. Police made hundreds of arrests.

In the first two weeks of July 2016, *The New York Times* counted 112 protests against police violence in eighty-eight cities. The following year, Republican legislators in many states responded to the growing protests by introducing fifty-six bills expanding the definitions of riot, criminal trespass, and obstruction of traffic. Many of these bills also increased the penalties for these offenses.[32]

In response to the Bayou Bridge Pipeline protest, the Louisiana legislature passed a law creating a new offense of "unauthorized entry of critical infrastructure," which threatened protesters who trespassed with a felony conviction and up to five years in jail.

Two United Nations observers warned against the danger of overreaction in a letter to the State Department. "A number of undemocratic bills have been proposed in state legislatures with the purpose or effect of criminalizing peaceful protests," they declared. State legislators introduced another fifty-four bills in 2018 and 2019. Fifteen states approved twenty-three new restrictions.[33]

The protests continued and widened to include people who had never demonstrated before. In March 2018, high school students across the country demonstrated against gun violence in response to the murder of seventeen students and faculty at Marjory Stoneman Douglas High School in Parkland, Florida. In the largest student-led demonstration since the Vietnam War, more than two hundred thousand young people and their supporters gathered in Washington to pressure Congress to adopt effective gun control legislation. Nearly a million students briefly walked out of class to show their support.

Yet even the national demonstrations by women and students and the hundreds of local protests organized under the umbrella of the Black Lives Matter movement could not prepare the country for the outpouring of anger that occurred on May 25, 2020.

Only six weeks after police killed Breonna Taylor, the death of George Floyd was deeply shocking. As bystanders begged for his life, Floyd slowly suffocated while police officer Derek Chauvin pinned him to the ground with a knee on the back of his neck.

The protest began in Minneapolis but quickly spread to the rest of the country, driven by a video that a young woman recorded of the last minutes of Floyd's life. Over the next five weeks, there were demonstrations against police violence in more than two thousand cities and towns in the United States and more than sixty countries. According to several polls, between fifteen and twenty-six million Americans reported participating in a protest, making the demonstrations the largest in American history.

They were also the most contentious. The men and women who took to the streets were furious at the police. Yet, with few exceptions, the protesters did not resort to violence. A study of seventy-seven hundred BLM demonstrations published in the fall of 2020 found that 93 percent were peaceful.[34]

The police were responsible for most of the violence. During the first week of the protest, police officers pushed and punched demonstrators and used tear gas, pepper spray, and rubber bullets to break up crowds. These tactics were on full display in Washington when police cleared peaceful protesters from Lafayette Square, a traditional site of protest in front of the White House, so President Trump could cross the square and have his picture taken standing in front of a church.

The *Guardian* newspaper documented more than a thousand instances of police brutality over the summer. There were certainly many more. Thirteen hundred people filed complaints against the

President Donald J. Trump walks from the White House to St. John's Episcopal Church, 2020

New York City Police Department, prompting the New York attorney general to sue police officials.[35]

During 2020, police officers also arrested or detained at least 117 reporters and photographers, and more than one-third were assaulted by police — beaten, hit with rubber bullets, or covered with tear gas. The overwhelming majority of the cases occurred during the George Floyd protests.[36]

Tens of thousands of peaceful protesters were arrested. *The Washington Post* reported more than seventeen thousand in just the first two weeks. Police charged the overwhelming majority with misdemeanors, including violating curfews and other emergency orders. For months, those facing charges wondered what would happen to them. In the end, prosecutors dismissed thousands of cases.[37]

Nevertheless, a year later, the millions who marched could take satisfaction in knowing that their protests had made a difference. The turnout was evidence of the breadth of support for change. Even at the height of the civil rights movement in the 1960s, most of the protesters were Black. The protests over the death of George Floyd were larger, more widespread, and ethnically much more diverse. Whites made up the majority of residents in 40 percent of the counties where marches occurred.

There was also evidence that the country was moving forward with reforms. By the fall, more than half of the nation's largest police departments had banned the use of choke holds and other neck restraints like the one that killed Floyd.

State and local governments were actively debating measures to increase police accountability, including modifying or eliminating qualified immunity, which gives officers the benefit of the doubt when they have committed a violent act during the course of an arrest. There were also proposals to strengthen the power of civilian review boards to oversee police conduct. In New York, Governor Andrew Cuomo issued an executive order making it easier to get access to a police officer's disciplinary record.

The achievements of the Black Lives Matter movement and the George Floyd protests extended beyond the issue of police violence, putting race relations at the center of public discourse for the first time in sixty years. The issue of inequality shaped every aspect of American life, including the policies of the new Democratic administration in Washington in 2021.

Many Americans had a different view of the public unrest. They saw the incidents of violence at the fringes of the protests, particularly those led by small numbers of menacing, black-suited anarchists, as evidence of an effort to destabilize the country.

Republican lawmakers responded with another burst of legislation to restrict the protests. They introduced more than a hundred bills during the spring and summer of 2021. Once again, only a handful of the proposed restrictions became law. The ones that did showed a clear animus toward the Black Lives Matter movement.[38]

Tennessee legislators were furious when protesters began camping on the grounds of the state capitol and demanded to meet with the governor. The governor refused and called a special session of the legislature, which passed a bill that threatened the sit-in participants with up to six years in prison and loss of the right to vote if they did not leave.

The legislators also did not like the fact that the demonstrators sometimes shouted at them as they came and went. They increased the penalty for interfering with a meeting of the legislature, including "verbal utterance," and banned the use of chalk to write on government property.

In a final expression of anger, the new law required that anyone arrested for a protest offense be held for at least twelve hours before being released on bail.

Florida passed a new law that was even more draconian. Governor Ron DeSantis claimed its target to be "professional agitators, bent on sowing disorder and causing mayhem in our cities," "crazed lunatics," and "scraggly looking antifa types." In fact, the law applies to all protesters, who are now subject to "vaguely defined offenses related to riot and so-called 'mob intimidation.'" It makes blocking traffic punishable by up to fifteen years in jail and provides limited immunity to someone who hurts a protester with a car.[39]

The ACLU and the NAACP have filed a lawsuit challenging

the Florida law on behalf of Black Lives Matter and several other civil rights groups, including Chainless Change. "Public protests have always been a core component of American movements that resulted in real change," Marq Mitchell, its CEO, said. "We are committed to doing our part to safeguard the First Amendment rights of Floridians."[40]

The surging movement for racial justice — and the effort to suppress it — affected every aspect of American society by the middle of 2021. As has happened so often in the past, schools became a major arena of conflict.

While the number of book challenges has declined since the 1980s, efforts to ban books continue to reflect the conflicts in American society. In 2019, seven of the ten most challenged books were about the lives of LGBTQ people. In 2020, six of the top ten addressed racial issues.[41]

By the middle of 2021, the concern over what to teach students about race had become a national controversy. Conservatives rejected the idea that racism remains a serious problem. In his final days in office, Trump issued an executive order banning "race or sex scapegoating" in training federal employees. This included suggesting "an individual, by virtue of his or her race or sex, bears responsibility for actions committed in the past by other members of the same race or sex."[42]

Biden canceled Trump's order, but the campaign to censor what can be said about race spread rapidly as conservative advocacy groups urged their supporters to pressure state legislators to take action. "We're getting lots of calls from all over the state, from parents in schools where they feel very uncomfortable with children coming home being exposed to things," a Republican legislator explained. "So when we hear that, we've got to address it."[43]

In the first half of 2021, legislators in sixteen states introduced bills that prohibited the teaching of critical race theory, an academic theory that holds that racism has strongly shaped American society and continues to handicap Black citizens. Some bills explicitly prohibited the use of a curriculum based on the 1619 Project, a historical study by *The New York Times* that takes its name from the year the first twenty enslaved Africans arrived in America.

In Tennessee, officials approved a law that cut off funding to public and charter schools teaching critical race theory. When questioned by reporters, supporters of the bill were unable to identify any school district where teachers are using it. The only evidence of a "problem" was an unverified report that a seven-year-old had come home from school and asked her mother: "Am I a racist?"

All of the Black members of the legislature expressed their opposition to the bill. Senator Katrina Robinson, a Democrat, said she was "deeply and profoundly offended by it." Robinson argued the Republican majority was opposed to all education about the history and impact of racism, pointing to the fact that she has been unable to gain support for a bill requiring Black history instruction in fifth and eighth grades.[44]

Representative Yusef Hakeem, another Black Democrat, asked John Ragan, the sponsor of the bill, if he believed systemic racism exists. Ragan did not respond, saying only that the term *systemic racism* does not appear in the bill.

The ACLU of Tennessee responded when supporters of the bill argued that it does not ban all discussion of racism but requires only that it be "impartial." "What does it mean to be impartial about slavery?" Heddy Weinberg, the executive director, and Brandon Tucker, the policy director, asked in an opinion piece in *The Tennessean*.[45]

"Should teachers avoid offering their perspectives or sharing those of others on slavery, policing, voting rights or racial justice?" they asked. "Will teachers be prohibited from providing a list of optional readings that may depart from the state's official interpretation of history?"

Apparently in response to this question, the final bill specified that teachers will not be limited in what they can say when they are responding to a student's question or referring to a historic figure or group.

However, the broader criticism leveled by the ACLU remained unanswered. Weinberg and Tucker recalled the history of the state capitol itself. When the building was under construction in 1845, budget constraints led the state to rent from a Tennessee slaveholder "fifteen or twenty likely, active, and intelligent negro men, to be quartered on public grounds."

"To build the temple of Tennessee's democracy, the state used the labor of the enslaved," they wrote. "This is our history. It is painful. But it is ours. . . . Acknowledging and learning from our past is part of the struggle to do better, to move us forward toward realizing the ideal that all people are created equal."

The ACLU fought one of its first battles against a Tennessee law banning the teaching of evolution. Once again, it was rejecting censorship. The battle for free speech continues.

CONCLUSION

Not long after my wife and I sat down for dinner in the summer of 2021 with our good friends Pat and Manny, I made Pat mad. The conversation turned to politics and then, inevitably, to the topic of misinformation. Pat wanted to know my position.

In searching for a quick answer, I told her that the First Amendment protects lies. This is not entirely true. In fact, a private individual or company can sue you for libel or defamation if you knowingly tell lies that damage their reputation. What I should have said is that it is not always possible to tell the truthfulness of a statement and that the Supreme Court has ruled that in order to protect the freedom to debate issues there must be "breathing room" for misstatements of fact.

Pat's question had caught me off guard, and I had responded defensively, but I think what really made her mad was the idea that we are powerless against the deadly lies that are spreading on social media.

I do not believe we are powerless against either misinformation or hate speech. On the contrary, I believe we have an obligation to fight them. But, like other civil libertarians, I don't think censorship is the solution. The best way to fight bad speech is with speech that calls out racist and sexist speech and exposes falsehoods.

Defenders of free speech are just as alarmed and frustrated as other Americans by blatant lies and bigotry. But legal restrictions have not worked in other countries. There is also a danger that suppression will drive extremists further underground, making them harder to fight.[1]

The most important reason for defending free speech for all, including those we fear or abhor, is that history shows the power of free speech to change things for the better. While we live in a country where injustice persists, the United States is a far more democratic country today than it was two hundred years ago or even sixty years ago.

Free speech alone does not deserve credit for the advance of social justice. It took a war to end slavery. However, it is hard to imagine abolition without the abolitionists who worked for more than thirty years to challenge the nation's deep-seated racism. The fight for equal rights for women owed a lot to improved educational and vocational opportunities, but women would not have won the vote without the fearless advocacy of women like Susan B. Anthony and Alice Paul.

The danger of censorship is that it gives government the power to suppress the very groups and individuals that are demanding their rights. Frederick Douglass knew this from personal experience. He never recovered the full use of his right hand following an attack by a pro-slavery mob. "The right of free speech is a very precious one, especially to the oppressed," Douglass said in 1854.[2]

A century later, police in Selma, Alabama, clubbed civil rights leader John Lewis into unconsciousness. Like other veterans of the movement, Congressman Lewis later paid tribute to the importance of free speech and freedom of the press. "If it hadn't been for the media, for brave, courageous journalists, the civil rights movement would have been like a bird without wings," he said.[3]

We are living through some dark days in America. However, in the wake of the Women's March, the #MeToo movement, the March for Our Lives, Black Lives Matter, and the George Floyd protests, there is reason for optimism. Two centuries of protest against injustice and untruths provide powerful support for the hope that American democracy will continue to grow.

NOTES

Chapter 1

1. Aleine Austin, *Matthew Lyon: "New Man" of the Democratic Revolution, 1749–1822* (University Park and London: Pennsylvania State University Press, 1981), 100.

2. Austin, *Matthew Lyon*.

3. Austin, *Matthew Lyon*, 77.

4. Austin, *Matthew Lyon*, 105.

5. An Act in Addition to the Act, Entitled "An Act for the Punishment of Certain Crimes Against the United States," 5th Cong, 2d Sess, ch 74 (1798).

6. Austin, *Matthew Lyon*, 107.

7. Austin, *Matthew Lyon*, 106.

8. Austin, *Matthew Lyon*, 110.

9. Austin, *Matthew Lyon*, 108.

10. Austin, *Matthew Lyon*, 119.

11. Geoffrey R. Stone, *Perilous Times: Free Speech in Wartime: From the Sedition Act of 1798 to the War on Terrorism* (New York: W. W. Norton, 2004), 46, 66.

12. Quoted in Brenda Wineapple, "Our First Authoritarian Crackdown," *New York Review of Books*, July 2, 2020, review of Wendell Bird, *Criminal Dissent: Prosecutions Under the Alien and Sedition Acts of 1798* (Cambridge, MA: Harvard University Press, 2020); Stone, *Perilous Times*, 61.

13. Austin, *Matthew Lyon*, 127.

14. Austin, *Matthew Lyon*, 128.

15. Stone, *Perilous Times*, 42.

16. *New York Times v. Sullivan*, 376 US 254, 270 (1964).

17. Benjamin Quarles, *Black Abolitionists* (New York: Oxford University Press, 1969), 4.

18. Quarles, *Black Abolitionists*, 7.

19. Quarles, *Black Abolitionists*.

20. Quarles, *Black Abolitionists*,17.

21. Henry Mayer, *All on Fire: William Lloyd Garrison and the Abolition of Slavery* (New York: St. Martin's Press, 1998; paperback edition, 2000), 84.

22. Mayer, *All on Fire*, 94.

23. Mayer, *All on Fire*, 110.

24. Mayer, *All on Fire*, 112.

25. Mayer, *All on Fire*, 120.

26. Mayer, *All on Fire*, 122, 123.

27. Mayer, *All on Fire*, 175.

28. Mayer, *All on Fire*, 127.

29. Mayer, *All on Fire*, 197.

30. Leonard L. Richards, "Gentlemen of Property and Standing": Anti-Abolition Mobs in Jacksonian America (New York: Oxford University Press, 1970), 12.

31. Mayer, *All on Fire*, 291.

32. Mayer, *All on Fire*, 203.

33. Russel B. Nye, *Fettered Freedom: Civil Liberties and the Slavery Controversy, 1830–1860* (East Lansing: Michigan State University Press, 1949), 35.

34. Nye, *Fettered Freedom*, 35–36.

35. Nye, *Fettered Freedom*, 38.

36. William Lee Miller, *Arguing About Slavery: The Great Battle in the United States Congress* (New York: Alfred A. Knopf, 1996) 229.

37. Quoted in Miller, *Arguing About Slavery*, 231.

38. Nye, *Fettered Freedom*, 104.

39. Nye, *Fettered Freedom*, 107.

40. Nye, *Fettered Freedom*, 115.

41. Paul Simon, *Lovejoy: Martyr to Freedom* (Saint Louis, MO: Concordia Publishing House, 1964), 131.

42. Simon, *Lovejoy*, 132.

43. Quarles, *Black Abolitionists*, 63.

44. David W. Blight, *Frederick Douglass: Prophet of Freedom* (New York: Simon & Schuster, 2018) 134.

45. Frederick Douglass, "The Kansas-Nebraska Bill," speech delivered in Chicago, October 30, 1854, Frederick Douglass Project Writings: The Kansas-Nebraska Bill, Frederick Douglass Project, University of Rochester, https://rbscp.lib.rochester.edu/4400.

46. Douglass, "The Kansas-Nebraska Bill."

47. "Frederick Douglass's 'Plea for Freedom of Speech in Boston [Dec. 9, 1860]," *Law and Liberty* (August 21, 2019), https://lawliberty.org/frederick-douglass-plea-for-freedom-of-speech-in-boston.

48. Eleanor Flexner and Ellen Fitzpatrick, *Century of Struggle: The Woman's Rights Movement in the United States* (Cambridge, MA: Harvard University Press, 1996, enlarged edition), 41.

49. Flexner and Fitzpatrick, *Century of Struggle*, 48.

50. Miller, *Arguing About Slavery*, 317.

51. Miller, *Arguing About Slavery*, 320.

52. Flexner and Fitzpatrick, *Century of Struggle*, 43.

53. Flexner and Fitzpatrick, *Century of Struggle*, 46.

54. Flexner and Fitzpatrick, *Century of Struggle*, 44.

55. Flexner and Fitzpatrick, *Century of Struggle*, 70.

56. Flexner and Fitzpatrick, *Century of Struggle*, 45.
57. Flexner and Fitzpatrick, *Century of Struggle*, 85.
58. Flexner and Fitzpatrick, *Century of Struggle*, 85–86.
59. Flexner and Fitzpatrick, *Century of Struggle*, 81.
60. Helen Lefkowitz Horowitz, *Rereading Sex: Battles Over Sexual Knowledge and Suppression in Nineteenth-Century America* (New York: Alfred A. Knopf, 2002), 414.
61. Roderick Bradford, *D. M. Bennett: The Truth Seeker* (Amherst, NY: Prometheus Books, 2006), passim.
62. David M. Rabban, *Free Speech in Its Forgotten Years* (Cambridge, UK: Cambridge University Press, 1997), 64.
63. Flexner and Fitzpatrick, *Century of Struggle*, 251.
64. Katherine H. Adams and Michael L. Keene, *Alice Paul and the American Suffrage Campaign* (Urbana and Chicago: University of Illinois Press, 2008), 12.
65. Adams and Keene, *Alice Paul and the American Suffrage Campaign*, 15.
66. Adams and Keene, *Alice Paul and the American Suffrage Campaign*, 97.

Chapter 2

1. Melvyn Dubofsky, *We Shall Be All: A History of the Industrial Workers of the World* (Urbana and Chicago: University of Illinois Press, 2000, abridged edition), 101.
2. Philip S. Foner, *The Industrial Workers of the World, 1905–1917* (New York: International Publishers, 1965, paperback edition), 179.
3. Foner, *The Industrial Workers of the World*.
4. Graham Adams Jr., *Age of Industrial Violence, 1910–1915: The Activities and Findings of the United States Commission on Industrial Relations* (New York: Columbia University Press, 1966), 216–17.
5. U.S. Commission on Industrial Relations, *Final Report and Testimony*, II:10873.
6. Elizabeth Gurley Flynn, *The Rebel Girl: An Autobiography; My First Life* (New York: International Publishers, 1973; new, revised edition, third printing, 1994), 107.
7. Flynn, *Rebel Girl*, 64.
8. Foner, *Industrial Workers of the World*, 182.
9. Flynn, *Rebel Girl*, 110.
10. Foner, *Industrial Workers of the World*, 182.
11. Harry N. Scheiber, *The Wilson Administration and Civil Liberties* (Ithaca, NY: Cornell University Press, 1960), 6.

12. David M. Rabban, "The Free Speech League, the ACLU, and Changing Conceptions of Free Speech in American History," *Stanford Law Review* 45, no. 47 (November 1992): 106.

13. Scheiber, *The Wilson Administration and Civil Liberties*, 33.

14. Dubofsky, *We Shall Be All*, 248.

15. Paul L. Murphy, *World War I and the Origin of Civil Liberties in the United States* (New York: W. W. Norton, 1979), 173.

16. Geoffrey R. Stone, *Perilous Times: Free Speech in Wartime: From the Sedition Act of 1798 to the War on Terrorism* (New York: W. W. Norton, 2004), 171.

17. *Debs v. US*, 249 US 211 (1919).

18. James R. Mock and Cedric Larson, *Words That Won the War: The Story of the Committee on Public Information, 1917–1919* (Princeton, NJ: Princeton University Press, 1939), 64.

19. Donald Johnson, *Challenge to American Freedom: World War I and the Rise of the American Civil Liberties Union* (Lexington: University of Kentucky Press, 1963), 65.

20. "Statement by Emma Goldman," October 27, 1919, Emma Goldman Papers, University of California–Berkeley, available at https://www.lib.berkeley.edu/goldman/pdfs/StatementbyEmmaGoldmanattheFederalHearingREportation.pdf.

21. "Statement by Emma Goldman."

22. *Shaffer v. US*, 255 F 886, 887–89 (9th Cir. 1919), quoted in Stone, *Perilous Times*, 171.

23. Jonathan Prude, "Portrait of a Civil Libertarian: The Faith and Fear of Zechariah Chafee, Jr.," *Journal of American History* 60, no. 3 (December 1973): 637.

24. Zechariah Chafee Jr., "Freedom of Speech," *New Republic* 17 (November 16, 1918): 67.

25. Chafee, "Freedom of Speech," 68.

26. *Schenck v. US*, 249 US 52 (1919).

27. Richard Polenberg, *Fighting Faiths: The Abrams Case, the Supreme Court and Free Speech* (New York: Viking Penguin, 1987; reprint New York: Penguin Books, 1989), 221.

28. Polenberg, *Fighting Faiths*, 236.

29. *Abrams v. US*, 250 US 616 (1919), 628.

30. *Abrams v. US*, 630.

31. "Reminiscences of Roger N. Baldwin," Oral History Collection, Columbia University, 16–17, 19.

32. "Reminiscences of Roger N. Baldwin," 153.

33. "Reminiscences of Roger N. Baldwin," 153.

34. "Reminiscences of Roger N. Baldwin," 4.

35. Samuel Walker, *In Defense of American Liberties: A History of the ACLU* (New York: Oxford University Press), 29.

36. Robert C. Cottrell, *Roger Nash Baldwin and the American Civil Liberties Union* (New York: Columbia University Press, 2000), 54, 59.

37. Walker, *In Defense of American Liberties*, 47.

38. Walker, *In Defense of American Liberties.*

39. Donald Johnson, "The American Civil Liberties Union: Origins, 1914–1917" (PhD dissertation, Columbia University, 1960), 306–8.

40. Arthur Garfield Hays, *Let Freedom Ring* (New York: Boni and Liveright, 1928), 105–6.

41. American Civil Liberties Union, *The Fight for Free Speech* (New York: American Civil Liberties Union, 1921), 15.

42. Albert DeSilver, "The Ku Klux Klan," *The Nation* (September 14, 192): 8.

43. Walker, *In Defense of American Liberties*, 61–62.

44. Walker, *In Defense of American Liberties*, 61.

45. Norman Hapgood, ed., *Professional Patriots* (New York: Albert & Charles Boni, 1928), 16–17.

46. Christopher M. Finan, *From the Palmer Raids to the Patriot Act: A History of the Fight for Free Speech in America* (Boston: Beacon Press, 2007), 61.

47. Edward J. Larson, *Summer for the Gods: The Scopes Trial and America's Continuing Debate Over Science and Religion* (Cambridge, MA: Harvard University Press, 1997; paperback edition, 1998), 112.

48. Charles Evans Hughes, "Liberty and Law," *American Bar Association Journal* (September 1925): 564–66.

49. Paul S. Boyer, *Purity in Print: The Vice-Society Movement and Book Censorship in America* (New York: Charles Scribner's Sons, 1968), 30.

50. Boyer, *Purity in Print*, 79.

51. Boyer, *Purity in Print*, 84.

52. Boyer, *Purity in Print*, 105.

53. *New York Times*, "Likely to Railroad Clean Books Bill," April 1, 1923, 1, 4.

54. Boyer, *Purity in Print*, 31.

55. Boyer, *Purity in Print*, 32.

56. Boyer, *Purity in Print*, 113.

57. Boyer, *Purity in Print*, 115.

58. Boyer, *Purity in Print*, 118.

59. Boyer, *Purity in Print*, 122.

60. Quoted in Boyer, *Purity in Print*, 183.

61. Boyer, *Purity in Print*, 187.

62. Boyer, *Purity in Print*, 188.

63. Boyer, *Purity in Print*, 188.

64. Boyer, *Purity in Print*, 203.

65. Boyer, *Purity in Print*, 241.
66. Boyer, *Purity in Print*, 204.
67. Boyer, *Purity in Print*, 198.
68. Boyer, *Purity in Print*, 199.
69. Judge Woolsey's opinion was reprinted in James Joyce, *Ulysses* (New York: Random House, 1961), x.

Chapter 3

1. Shaw Francis Peters, *Judging Jehovah's Witnesses: Religious Persecution and the Dawn of the Rights Revolution* (Lawrence: University of Kansas Press, 2000), 26.
2. Peters, *Judging Jehovah's Witnesses*, 26.
3. Peters, *Judging Jehovah's Witnesses*, 71.
4. Peters, *Judging Jehovah's Witnesses*, 75.
5. *West Virginia State Board of Education v. Barnette*, 319 US 624 (1943), 642.
6. William O. Douglas, "The Black Silence of Fear," *New York Times Magazine* (January 13, 1952): 24.
7. Louise S. Robbins, *Censorship and the American Library: The American Library Association's Response to Threats to Intellectual Freedom, 1939-1969* (Westport, CT, and London: Greenwood Press, 1996), 71.
8. Robbins, *Censorship and the American Library*, 64.
9. "The Library's Bill of Rights (1939)," quoted in Robbins, *Censorship and the American Library*, 13.
10. Robbins, *Censorship and the American Library*, 13.
11. Robbins, *Censorship and the American Library*, 15.
12. "The Library Bill of Rights (1948)," quoted in Robbins, *Censorship and the American Library*, 35.
13. Robbins, *Censorship and the American Library*, 13.
14. Louise S. Robbins, *The Dismissal of Miss Ruth Brown: Civil Rights, Censorship and the American Library* (Norman: University of Oklahoma, 2000), 72.
15. Robbins, *The Dismissal of Miss Ruth Brown*, 163.
16. "Statement on Labeling (1951)," quoted in Robbins, *Censorship and the American Library*, 53.
17. Robbins, *Censorship and the American Library*, 77.
18. American Library Association, "The Freedom to Read," *Intellectual Freedom Manual*, 7th ed. (Chicago: American Library Association, 2000): 228.
19. Robbins, *Censorship and the American Library*, 78.
20. Robbins, *Censorship and the American Library*, 80.
21. *Yates v. US*, 354 US 298, 324-25 (1957).

22. *Roth v. US*, 354 US 476, 487 (1957).

23. Taylor Branch, *Parting the Waters: America in the King Years, 1954–1963* (New York: Simon & Schuster, 1988; reprint, New York: Touchstone, 1989), 140.

24. Branch, *Parting the Waters*, 141.

25. "Southern Manifesto" (1956), https://d1exzaozk4q6za.cloudfront.net/history/am-docs/southern-manifesto.pdf.

26. "Arkansas Loses in NAACP Case," *New York Times* (June 9, 1959): 31.

27. *New York Times v. Sullivan*, 376 US 254, 270, 273, 274 (1964).

28. Anthony Lewis, *Make No Law: The Sullivan Case and the First Amendment* (New York: Random House, 1991), 154.

29. James Miller, "Democracy in the Streets": *From Port Huron to the Siege of Chicago* (New York: Simon & Schuster, 1987), 44.

30. Miller, "Democracy in the Streets," 49.

31. Miller, "Democracy in the Streets," 124–25.

32. David Lance Goines, *The Free Speech Movement: Coming of Age in the 1960s* (Berkeley, CA: Ten Speed Press, 1993), 168.

33. Margot Adler, "My Life in the Free Speech Movement: Memories of a Freshman," in Robert Cohen and Reginald E. Zelnick, *The Free Speech Movement: Reflections on Berkeley in the 1960's* (Berkeley: University of California Press, 2002), 125.

34. Stone, *Perilous Times*, 442.

35. Richard Gid Powers, *Broken: The Troubled Past and Uncertain Future of the FBI* (New York: Free Press, 2004), 246–47.

36. Powers, *Broken*, 279.

37. *Brandenburg v. Ohio*, 395 US 444, 444–45.

38. *Brandenburg v. Ohio*, 447.

39. Harold L. Cross, *The People's Right to Know: Legal Access to Public Records and Proceedings* (New York: Columbia University Press, 1953), xiii.

Chapter 4

1. E. R. Hutchinson, *Tropic of Cancer on Trial: A Case History of Censorship* (New York: Grove Press, 1968), 244.

2. Fred Strebeigh, "Defining Law on the Feminist Frontier," *New York Times Magazine* (October 6, 1991): 31.

3. *American Booksellers Association v. Hudnut*, 598 F. Supp. 1316 (1984), 1337.

4. Teller, "Movies Don't Cause Crime," *New York Times* (January 17, 1992).

5. Ad Hoc Committee of Feminists for Free Expression to members of the US Senate Judiciary Committee, undated [February 1992], 1.

6. Robert O'Harrow Jr., "Six Weeks in Autumn," *Washington Post* (October 27, 2002): W06.

7. Emily Eakin, "On the Lookout for Patriotic Incorrectness," *New York Times* (November 24, 2001): 15.

8. Jim Lobe, "War on Dissent Widens," *Foreign Policy in Focus* (March 1, 2002), https://fpif.org/the_war_on_dissent_widens/.

9. USA Patriot Act, Section 215, 50 USC 1861.

10. Northampton, Massachusetts, City Council Resolution, May 2, 2002.

11. ACLU press release, October 16, 2002, http://www.aclu.org/safefree/general/17665prs20021016.html.

12. *Burlington Free Press* (December 21, 2002): 1B.

13. *The Tennessean* (January 25, 2003); American Library Association, "Resolution on the USA PATRIOT Act and Related Measures That Infringe on the Rights of Library Users" (January 29, 2003).

14. Eric Lichtblau, "Ashcroft Mocks Librarians and Others Who Oppose Parts of Counterterrorism Law," *New York Times* (September 16, 2003): 23.

15. Timothy C. Shiell, *Campus Hate Speech on Trial* (Lawrence: University Press of Kansas, 1998), 18.

16. Shiell, *Campus Hate Speech on Trial*, 19.

17. Samuel Walker, *Hate Speech: The History of an American Controversy* (Lincoln and London: University of Nebraska Press, 1994), 150.

18. *RAV v. St. Paul*, 505 US 377 (1992).

19. "Shouting Down a Lecture," *Inside Higher Education* (March 3, 2017), https://www.insidehighered.com/news/2017/03/03/middlebury-students-shout-down-lecture-charles-murray.

20. "Justices, 5–4, Reject Corporate Spending Limit," *New York Times* (January 21, 2010).

21. *Citizens United v. Federal Election Commission*, 558 US 310 (2010).

22. "Remarks of President Barack Obama — State of the Union Address as Delivered" (January 13, 2010), https://obamawhitehouse.archives.gov/the-press-office/2016/01/12/remarks-president-barack-obama-%E2%80%93-prepared-delivery-state-union-address.

23. "Supreme Court Deals Blow to Public-Sector Unions, Ruling Against 'Fair-Share' Fees," *The Hill* (June 27, 2018), https://thehill.com/regulation/court-battles/39437-court-deals-blow-to-public-sector-unions-ruling-against-fair-share?rl=1.

24. Alex Greenberger, "'The Painting Must Go': Hannah Black . . . ," *Art News* (March 21, 201), https://www.artnews.com/artnews/news/the-painting-must-go-hannah-black-pens-open-letter-to-the-whitney-about-controversial-biennial-work-7992/.

25. "Editor's Note," *The Nation* (July 5, 2018), https://www.thenation.com/article/archive/how-to/.

NOTES

26. Juliana Kaplan, *Business Insider* (June 8, 2020), https://www.businessinsider.com/publishing-workers-calling-out-from-work-for-day-of-action-2020-6.

27. "A Letter on Justice and Open Debate," *Harper's Magazine* (July 7, 2020), https://harpers.org/a-letter-on-justice-and-open-debate/.

28. "A More Specific Letter on Justice and Open Debate," *The Objective* (July 10, 2020), https://www.objectivejournalism.org/p/a-more-specific-letter-on-justice.

29. "Simon & Schuster Statement Regarding the Tyranny of Big Tech by Josh Hawley" (January 7, 2021), http://about.simonandschuster.biz/news/josh-hawley/.

30. A. J. Perez, "Donald Trump: NFL Players' Anthem Protests a Lack of Respect for Our Country" (September 12, 2016), https://www.usatoday.com/story/sports/nfl/2016/09/12/national-anthem-protests-donald-trump-kaepernick-dolphins-foster/90254600/.

31. "Transcript: Donald Trump's Comments About Women," *New York Times* (October 8, 2016), https://www.nytimes.com/2016/10/08/us/donald-trump-tape-transcript.html.

32. PEN America, "Arresting Dissent: Legislative Restrictions on the Right to Protest" (May 2020): 4.

33. PEN America, "Arresting Dissent," 8.

34. "93% of Black Lives Matter Protests Have Been Peaceful, New Report Finds," *Time* (September 5, 2020), https://time.com/5886348/report-peaceful-protests/.

35. "Nearly 1,000 Instances of Police Brutality Recorded in US Anti-Racism Protests," *The Guardian* (October 29, 2020), https://www.theguardian.com/us-news/2020/oct/29/us-police-brutality-protest; "New York State Sues NYPD Over Its Handling of 2020 Racial Justice Protests," NPR (January 14, 2021), https://www.npr.org/2021/01/14/956793786/new-york-state-sues-nypd-over-its-handling-of-2020-racial-justice-protests.

36. "A Record Breaking Number of Journalists Arrested This Year," Freedom of the Press Foundation (December 14, 2020), https://freedom.press/news/2020-report-journalists-arrested-us/.

37. "Arrested George Floyd Protesters Most Often Charged," *Washington Post* (October 23, 2020), https://www.washingtonpost.com/graphics/2020/investigations/george-floyd-protesters-arrests; "Why Charges Against Protesters Are Being Dismissed by the Thousands," *New York Times* (February 11, 2021), https://www.nytimes.com/2020/11/19/us/protests-lawsuits-arrests.html.

38. PEN America, "Closing Ranks: State Legislators Deepen Assault on the Right to Protest" (2021), https://pen.org/closing-ranks-state-legislators-deepen-assaults-on-the-right-to-protest/.

39. PEN America, "Closing Ranks."

40. ACLU of Florida, "Civil Rights Groups File Federal Lawsuit Challenging Florida's Anti-Protest Law" (May 11, 2021), https://www.aclufl.org/en/press-releases/civil-rights-groups-file-federal-lawsuit-challenging-floridas-anti-protest-law.

41. "Top 10 Most Challenged Books Lists," Office for Intellectual Freedom, American Library Association, https://www.ala.org/advocacy/bbooks/frequentlychallengedbooks/top10.

42. "President Trump Issues Executive Order Prohibiting 'Divisive Concepts' in Federal Contractor Trainings," *Inside Government Contracts* (September 29, 2020), https://www.insidegovernmentcontracts.com/2020/09/president-trump-issues-executive-order-prohibiting-divisive-concepts-in-federal-contractor-trainings/.

43. "Tennessee Republicans Want to Withhold Funding from Schools Teaching Critical Race Theory," *The Tennessean* (May 2, 2021, updated May 3), https://www.tennessean.com/story/news/politics/2021/05/03/tennessee-gop-takes-critical-race-theory-lessons-inequality/7411907002/.

44. "Tennessee Bans Public Schools from Teaching Critical Race Theory Amid National Debate" (May 5, 2021), https://www.tennessean.com/story/news/politics/2021/05/05/tennessee-bans-critical-race-theory-schools-withhold-funding/4948306001/.

45. Heddy Weinberg and Brandon Tucker, "If Gov. Bill Lee OKs Critical Race Theory Ban, Tennessee Will Whitewash History," *The Tennessean* (May 19, 2021), https://www.tennessean.com/story/opinion/2021/05/19/if-gov-lee-bans-critical-race-theory-tennessee-whitewashes-history/5164949001/.

Conclusion

1. Nadine Strossen, *HATE: Why We Should Resist It with Free Speech, Not Censorship* (New York: Oxford University Press, 2018), passim.

2. Frederick Douglass, "The Kansas-Nebraska Bill," speech delivered in Chicago, October 30, 1854, Frederick Douglass Project Writings: The Kansas-Nebraska Bill, Frederick Douglass Project, University of Rochester, https://rbscp.lib.rochester.edu/4400.

3. Robbyn Mitchel, "Reporters Risked Life and Limb to Cover Civil Rights Movement," Poynter, https://www.poynter.org/news-release/2016/reporters-risked-life-and-limb-to-cover-civil-rights-movement/.

ACKNOWLEDGMENTS

I have the very good fortune of working for the National Coalition Against Censorship, an alliance of national literary, artistic, religious, educational, professional, labor, and civil liberties groups that has engaged in direct advocacy and education to support First Amendment principles for almost 50 years. I am grateful for the support of Jon Anderson, our board chair, and the other passionate and committed members of the board. The NCAC staff is both talented and hard working. It is a privilege to be a member of the team.

I also want to express my thanks to everyone at Steerforth Press. Chip Fleischer, the publisher, encouraged me to write this book and then edited it with skill. The rest of the staff is energetic, creative, and a pleasure to know. My thanks to David Goldberg, Anthony LaSasso, Helga Schmidt and Devin Wilkie.

As always, I am grateful for the support of my agent, Jill Marr.

ALSO AVAILABLE FROM **T2P** TRUTH TO POWER BOOKS

▌ DOCUMENTARY NARRATIVES